Institutional Violence and Disability

"This was several times with that damn cribbage board. I hate cribbage boards to this very day. They never beat us on the arms or legs or stuff, it was always on the bottom of the feet, I couldn't figure it out."

Brian L., Huronia Regional Centre Survivor

Over the past two decades, the public has borne witness to ongoing revelations of shocking, intense, and even sadistic forms of violence in spaces meant to provide care. This has been particularly true in institutions designed to care for people with disabilities. In this work, the authors not only *describe* institutional violence, but work to make sense of how and why institutional violence within care settings is both so pervasive and so profound.

Drawing on a wide range of primary data, including oral histories of institutional survivors and staff, ethnographic observation, legal proceedings and archival data, this book asks: What does institutional violence look like in practice and how might it be usefully categorized? How have extreme forms violence and neglect come to be the cultural norm across institutions? What organizational strategies in institutions foster the abdication of personal morality and therefore violence? How is institutional care the crucial "first step" in creating a culture that accepts violence as the norm?

This highly interdisciplinary work develops scholarly analysis of the history and importance of institutional violence and, as such, is of particular interest to scholars whose work engages with issues of disability, health care law and policy, violence, incarceration, organizational behaviour, and critical theory.

Kate Rossiter is an Associate Professor in the Department of Health Studies at Wilfrid Laurier University's Brantford campus, and is the Principal Investigator of "Recounting Huronia: An Arts-Based Participatory Research Project." Kate's background combines the critical social scientific study of public health and embodiment with theatre and performance studies. Kate lives in Brantford, Ontario with her partner and two children.

Jen Rinaldi is an Assistant Professor in the Legal Studies Program at the University of Ontario Institute of Technology. Her research takes up how non-normative— particularly cripped, Mad, fat, and queer—bodies are read, marked, and produced in and through socio-legal discourse. She explores these themes using collaborative and narrative-based methodologies and community arts praxis. Jen lives in Toronto, Ontario.

Routledge Advances in Disability Studies

Intellectual Disability and Being Human
A Care Ethics Model
Chrissie Rogers

The Changing Disability Policy System
Active Citizenship and Disability in Europe Volume 1
*Edited by Rune Halvorsen, Bjørn Hvinden, Jerome Bickenbach,
Delia Ferri and Ana Marta Guillén Rodriguez*

Citizenship Inclusion and Intellectual Disability
Biopolitics Post-Institutionalisation
Niklas Altermark

Intellectual Disability and the Right to a Sexual Life
A Continuation of the Autonomy/Paternalism Debate
Simon Foley

The Changing Disability Policy System
Active Citizenship and Disability in Europe Volume 2
*Edited by Rune Halvorsen, Bjørn Hvinden, Jerome Bickenbach,
Delia Ferri and Ana Marta Guillén Rodriguez*

Cultural Disability Studies in Education
Interdisciplinary Navigations of the Normative Divide
David Bolt

Institutional Violence and Disability
Punishing Conditions
Kate Rossiter and Jen Rinaldi

https://www.routledge.com/Routledge-Advances-in-Disability-Studies/
book-series/RADS

Institutional Violence and Disability

Punishing Conditions

Kate Rossiter and Jen Rinaldi

LONDON AND NEW YORK

First published 2019
by Routledge
2 Park Square, Milton Park, Abingdon, Oxon OX14 4RN

and by Routledge
52 Vanderbilt Avenue, New York, NY 10017, USA

First issued in paperback 2020

Routledge is an imprint of the Taylor & Francis Group, an informa business

© 2019 Kate Rossiter and Jen Rinaldi

The right of Kate Rossiter and Jen Rinaldi to be identified as authors of this work has been asserted by them in accordance with sections 77 and 78 of the Copyright, Designs and Patents Act 1988.

All rights reserved. No part of this book may be reprinted or reproduced or utilised in any form or by any electronic, mechanical, or other means, now known or hereafter invented, including photocopying and recording, or in any information storage or retrieval system, without permission in writing from the publishers.

Trademark notice: Product or corporate names may be trademarks or registered trademarks, and are used only for identification and explanation without intent to infringe.

British Library Cataloguing-in-Publication Data
A catalogue record for this book is available from the British Library

Library of Congress Cataloging-in-Publication Data
Names: Rossiter, Kate, author. | Rinaldi, Jennifer, author.
Title: Institutional violence and disability: punishing conditions /
Kate Rossiter and Jen Rinaldi.
Description: Abingdon, Oxon; New York, NY: Routledge,
2018. | Series: Routledge advances in disability studies |
Includes bibliographical references.
Identifiers: LCCN 2018014076 | ISBN 9781138495982 (hardback) |
ISBN 9781351022828 (pbk.)
Subjects: LCSH: People with disabilities—Institutional care. |
People with disabilities—Abuse of. | People with disabilities—
Violence against. | Institutional care—Moral and ethical aspects.
Classification: LCC HV1568 .R67 2018 | DDC 362.4/0485—dc23
LC record available at https://lccn.loc.gov/2018014076

ISBN 13: 978-0-367-58726-0 (pbk)
ISBN 13: 978-1-138-49598-2 (hbk)

Typeset in Times New Roman
by codeMantra

Contents

List of figures		vi
Acknowledgements		vii
1	Introduction	1
2	The Institutional Cases and the conditions for moral abdication	23
3	The institutional violence continuum	39
4	Thoughtlessness and violence as work culture	56
5	Quantifying and re-inscribing violence	67
6	Embedded trauma and embodied resistance	77
7	Conclusion	94
	Bibliography	103
	Index	109

List of figures

1.1 This undated postcard shows a bucolic image of the Orillia Asylum for Idiots (later renamed the Huronia Regional Centre) in its infancy 10

1.2 An image of a window looking out from Huronia's decrepit "K" cottage, covered in wire caging material. A small sticker on the window reads "no justice, no peace" 12

1.3 An image of a cage-like "crib cot" used to hold children and adults with severe physical disabilities taken at Huronia following its closure. Crib cots featured bars on all four sides as well on top to prevent residents from climbing out, and thus represent another form of isolation within the institution 17

1.4 An image of a bath thermometer used at the Huronia Regional Centre in order to discern the correct temperature for punitive ice baths 17

3.1 An image from the Huronia Regional Centre of a "side room" – a space in the institution used for the solitary confinement of residents, sometimes for days at a time 48

3.2 An underground tunnel in the Huronia Regional Centre that linked multiple buildings across the campus. Survivors describe sadistic violence occurring in the tunnel system 51

5.1 An undated Canadian eugenic-era educational leaflet describing and identifying four types of mental deficiencies 68

6.1 Huronia class action lawsuit lead Plaintiff Patricia Seth holding an adult-sized strait jacket, taken at the institution following its closure 78

6.2 A dilapidated former "playroom" at the Huronia Regional Centre. Survivors describe hours of monotony punctuated with episodes of violence occurring in these spaces 78

Acknowledgements

We would like to acknowledge with gratitude the financial support of the Social Sciences and Humanities Research Council of Canada's Insight Development Grant program and Wilfrid Laurier's Internal Grants program.

We would also like to acknowledge the Canadian Journal of Disability Studies and the edited collection Madness, Violence and Power: A Radical Anthology, which feature material used in this book.

To our colleagues, nancy viva davis halifax, David Fancy, Kim Jackson, Alex Tigchelaar, and Annalise Clarkson, whose creativity and thoughtful insights provided fertile theoretical ground for this work.

To my mom, for being my first and most enthusiastic reader (KR).

To our partners, Charlie and Nippe, whose deep patience and kindness have reminded us to care for ourselves as we've attended to the pain of others.

This book would not exist without the bravery, compassion, and wisdom of the *Recounting Huronia* team of survivors and allies, whose accounts of survival pushed us to think hard and do better.

To John Rossiter, whose quiet struggle didn't need words in order to be heard.

1 Introduction

"If you weren't retarded going in, you were fucking retarded coming out."
Pam, Huronia Survivor

In 2010, former residents of the Huronia Regional Centre, a total institution designed to warehouse people with intellectual disabilities, launched a landmark class action lawsuit against the government of Ontario. The government, they alleged, failed to protect and care for them during their time incarcerated at Huronia. Consequently, they endured years of profound neglect, violent and degrading forms of punishment, and, in some cases, sadistic levels of sexual and physical violence. As the class action lawsuit was prepared for court, Huronia survivors came forward to tell their stories. Some told of severe beatings that left behind a legacy of chronic pain and further disablement. Others spoke of routine humiliation at the hands of staff, such as being forced to "dig worms" – a punishment where residents were forced to lie on the floor with their hands behind their back, often with their face in a plate of food. Others, still, recounted childhood sexual abuse that took place on locked wards in bathrooms, closets, and offices. Some former residents of the Huronia Regional Centre were not able to say anything at all because trauma had rendered their memories shadowy and out of reach; because they were non-verbal to begin with; because they had not survived the institution at all and lay buried in unmarked graves on the institutional grounds.

In many ways, this story is neither surprising nor unusual. Over the past two decades, the public has borne witness to ongoing revelations regarding institutional violence. Such revelations have emerged from psychiatric facilities (Reaume, 1997), orphanages (Sherr, Roberts & Gandhi, 2017), residential and boarding schools (Castellano, Archibald & DeGagné, 2008; Mosby & Galloway, 2017), retirement homes (Chima, 1998) and institutions for persons with physical and intellectual disabilities (Malacrida, 2015; Rossiter & Clarkson, 2013). Common to all of these sites are two features. First, they are places ostensibly designed to provide care for people deemed vulnerable. Second, in each of these sites profound, and even sadistic, forms

2   Introduction

of violence have been inflicted on residents. Often, it is these extreme and shocking instances of violence that capture the public imagination and media focus, in particular sexual and other forms of brutal physical abuse, especially since such instances seem so distinct and unrelated to the act of caregiving proposed by the institution itself. However, to focus solely on extreme instances of violence is to miss the very fertile groundwork laid by more routine, mundane forms of daily violence that are central to the operation of institutional care. Instead, we collectively wonder *how* such extreme forms of violence take place, and *why* they happen with such regularity.

Institutional Violence and Disability: Punishing Conditions takes seriously the widespread problem of institutional violence and explores the issue of institutional violence in depth, particularly as it pertains to histories of disability. Rather than focusing on small-scale or individual assessments as a means of understanding institutional violence, we focus broadly on its many instances, iterations, and intensities, in order to describe the problem of institutional violence adequately and to identify social and organizational patterns that may lead to its ubiquity.

Understanding the roots of institutional violence, and its lasting effects, is crucial for two reasons. First, much of the Western world has a long history of incarcerating populations deemed unruly or in need of management under the guise of care provision. This includes people labelled as having a developmental or intellectual disability, Indigenous peoples, orphans, people coping with psychiatric disability, immigrants and refugees, and the elderly. People who have experienced institutionalization return to mainstream, non-institutional society carrying the oft-invisible burden of institutional violence, which may manifest itself as post-traumatic stress disorder (PTSD), depression, anxiety, enduring physical pain and disablement, addiction, or the inability to get or maintain education or employment. We bear the collective responsibility for responding to individuals who have experienced institutional violence.

Second, while some large-scale institutions have been closed, some have not, or have been replaced with similar care situations. This is to say, institutionalization is still a common practice, particularly in communities already marginalized by disability, race/immigration and socio-economic status. Further, societal attention has shifted focus from the ostensible provision of care for 'needy' populations to the punitive incarceration of criminalized populations. Importantly, however, *these populations may be one and the same*. While crime rates have dropped over the past two decades, prison populations are growing, and contain disproportionately large numbers of people with developmental and psychiatric disabilities as well as Indigenous and racialized people – populations that have historically been forced into incarceration due to perceived need rather than criminality. Thus, it is imperative to have a clear analysis regarding how and why institutional violence prevails.

Shockingly, while patterns of institutional violence are clear, little scholarly work exists that endeavours to explain how and why institutional

Introduction 3

violence seems to occur with such regularity. In fact, much literature pertaining to institutional violence focuses on violence enacted against *staff* by *institutional residents*. We ask: what kinds of organizational structures obliterate everyday moral codes and make way for extreme violence? How and why does caregiving itself comprise a necessary category of violence? What kinds of social and psychic mechanisms allow staff to erase or disavow their own practices of violence? Finally, how is institutional violence inscribed in and on the lives and bodies of those who have been incarcerated, and how do these inscriptions reassert forms of institutional practice over a lifespan, even after one has left the institution?

In this introductory chapter, we provide an overview of the problem of institutional violence. To do so, we provide a short discussion of what we mean by institutional violence, the ways in which institutional violence has been treated in scholarly literature so far, and why we believe institutional violence is a pressing social issue. We then provide an overview of the history of disability and institutionalization, with particular focus on Canadian history, and making connections to similar histories in both the United States and the United Kingdom. Following this overview, we turn to our own work and describe the methods and data we use to make our arguments. Specifically, this highly interdisciplinary work draws from multiple forms of data, including case law, oral history, and ethnographic observation; and multiple forms of analysis, including legal and discourse analysis, to thoroughly engage the topic at hand.

What is institutional violence?

What *is* institutional violence? For the purposes of this work, we rely on a broad definition. This is partly because we want to capture the nuances of this sort of violence, and partly because we believe extreme forms of violence, such as rape and battery, are connected to smaller and seemingly more mundane forms of violence, such as routine instances of verbal humiliation. Thus, we qualify institutional violence as *all* practices of humiliation, degradation, neglect, and abuse inflicted upon institutional residents, regardless of intention or circumstance. It is all too easy to dismiss institutional violence as a relic of past social attitudes toward disability and difference, or the unpleasant by-product of a difficult job, or the sign of a badly run institution. We propose instead that, while institutional violence is never acceptable, institutions themselves are *inherently* violent in form. We believe that practices of incarceration are in and of themselves violent, and necessarily produce further violence. To this end, we believe that other forms of care are not only possible, but absolutely critical as a project of justice.

Drawing from Goffman's (2007) seminal work regarding asylums, our work focuses on total institutions, which he describes as "a place of residence and work where a large number of like-situated individuals cut off from the wider society for an appreciable period of time together lead an

4 *Introduction*

enclosed formally administered round of life" (p. 11). In other words, total institutions are residential facilities separated from communities, where persons are committed to live, sleep, and perform all daily activities including work and school. Residents are subjected to around the clock surveillance, cannot leave without permission, and may live in the facility for prolonged periods of time: months, years, even lifetimes. While this definition could include jails and other detention centres, our work particularly focuses on institutions designed for *care* rather than *punishment*. This is not because violence does not occur in places like jails and detention centres – it does, with great regularity and intensity. Our definition is narrow because the fact that these spaces are designed for punishment and remediation makes the violence more socially palatable. However ugly this sentiment might be, there is some sense that those who end up in jails deserve violence or are more likely to perpetuate it. We, of course, vehemently disagree, but in order to circumvent such argumentation, we focus here only on institutions ostensibly designed for care.

Goffman's definition, and our resultant analysis, also leaves out places like group homes and halfway houses. Again, we believe that these are spaces in which violence occurs with some regularity, although there may be differences in terms of how, when, and how often such violence occurs. As such, they are worthy of further investigation and critical attention. However, our interest here is in understanding the dynamics of total institutions that are productive of violence so that survivors of such institutions are better understood and so that these kinds of institutions are closed for good and not built again.

Historical overview

While this work focuses broadly on the centrality of violence against people with disabilities in institutions, much of the source material comes particularly from the study of institutions designed to warehouse people with developmental or intellectual disabilities, psychiatric disabilities, and physical disabilities such as seeing and hearing impairments. Some of these institutions have been closed, yet others remain open or have been replaced with similar caregiving situations. These institutions bear the weight of historical attitudes regarding the treatment of disability, difference, and vulnerability. It is therefore important to understand how such institutions came to be, what they meant to accomplish, and how they were run. While this historical overview focuses on institutions in Canada, and particularly Ontario, the legacy of institutionalization is remarkably similar across the United States, the United Kingdom, Australia, and beyond (e.g., Johnson & Traustadóttir, 2005). Further, this historical overview is particularly concerned with custodial institutions for people diagnosed as having an intellectual disability, but growth of such institutions was concomitant with, and similar to, the design and development of institutions for people with other diagnoses, in particular those who were

Introduction 5

considered 'insane,' 'deaf,' or 'blind.' Finally, a historical overview necessitates using previously entrenched language for clarity's sake, though we recognize much of the terminology is dated, and has fallen out of use because it has been found inaccurate or even degrading.

Institutionalization and disability

The modern rise of the state wrought many changes in terms of understanding and caring for those perceived as vulnerable. One such change has been the development of large-scale, state-run institutions such as hospitals and asylums. In Canada, institutions were placed under provincial control and management following the confederation of Canadian provinces in 1867 (Park, 1990). In Ontario, the Department of Provincial Secretary was responsible for asylums, charities, prisons, and public institutions until 1931, when responsibilities were transferred to, and shared by, the newly created Departments of Health and Public Works.

By the mid-nineteenth century, the treatment of people with disabilities increasingly fell under the purview of science and medicine, and thus diagnosis, classification, and treatment of people with perceived disabilities became an occupying concern. The development of medical practice, pedagogical notions of "physiological treatment" (see Stuckey, 2013, p. 237), and rehabilitation sciences ushered in the development of new methods of treating and educating 'deaf,' 'dumb,' 'blind,' 'idiot,' and other 'backward' children based on seemingly indisputable models of biological deficiency (Williston, 1971).

In Canada, the impact of socially legitimized scientific testing and resultant diagnoses led to the growth of specialized institutions such as the Orillia Asylum for Idiots, as well as schools for deaf and blind children, such as W. Ross MacDonald School for the Blind in Brantford and the Institut Raymond-Dewar for deaf and hard of hearing students in Montréal. Urban centres such as Toronto established education systems based on new "scientific methods of intelligence testing," which helped to rank and separate 'defective' children, calling on and perpetuating the popular notion that disability and 'feeble-mindedness' was an increasing urban threat (Chupik & Wright, 2006, p. 80). The diagnostic procedures that identified many individuals as in need of institutional care paved the way for later justifications for violent treatment. Williston (1971), for example, argued in a report identifying institutional conditions that early beliefs regarding the diagnosis and care of people with intellectual disabilities in Canada caused three damaging institutional tendencies that remained throughout their existence: isolation, overcrowding, and perpetual cost containment. The report characterized these early trends at such institutions as paving the way for much larger issues including gross neglect and maltreatment – issues that form the backbone of the allegations laid in recent class action lawsuits.

6   *Introduction*

Ontario's institutions were founded with optimistic, yet nonetheless marginalizing, beliefs regarding the segregated care of people with disability. Stuckey (2013) argues that the Victorian-era "medico-pedagogic method" (p. 237) that informed the growth of institutions in North America at this time was based on progressive ideals of well-rounded education for people with disability. Armstrong (2002) locates the growth of vocational training within the bureaucratic development of asylums and workhouses as a method of rendering institutionalized populations both productive and controllable. Similarly, residential schools for deaf and blind children were established across North America throughout the nineteenth century with the intention of lifting the 'afflicted classes' of deaf and blind children out of poverty and social reliance through punitive forms of vocational training alongside the regular educational curriculum. Deaf children were entreated to particularly restrictive forms of treatment-based education following an 1880 ban on the use of sign language deaf classrooms in favour of oralism – that is, lip reading and vocal articulation. Deaf children who persisted in using American Sign Language (ASL) were punished with physical abuse and restraint, including at schools in Canada (Baynton, 1998).

These views stand in contrast with earlier beliefs, which perceived disability as a social, legal, and even religious concern, but not a concern of medicine or education: "It was considered a regrettable and incurable condition about which medical practitioners, both orthodox and unorthodox, could do little" (Wright, 2011, p. 28). Thus, given pervasive views regarding the treatment of people with disability, Ontario care-related policies during the early twentieth century generally promoted segregated, custodial care within closed institutions (Park, 1990) for the twinned purposes of education of people with disabilities, and, in the case of psychiatric and intellectual disability, for the putative protection of the broader society (Park, 1990; Williston, 1971).

From their inception, life within Canadian institutions was unrelentingly oppressive; however, many years of financial strain, provincial neglect, chronic overcrowding, and prevailing cultural attitudes of fear, abjection, and the need for social isolation left institutional residents vulnerable to widespread abuse. Staff frequently used physical abuse as forms of punishment (Stewart & Russell, 2001). As early as 1906, C.K. Clarke, Superintendent of the Toronto Hospital for the Insane, claimed that amenities such as toilets and bathing facilities were "a menace to the health of the inmates" (Reaume, 1997, p. 79). Secluded areas "between doors" or "cross hall" were used to hide abuses from incoming family or friends who were often abruptly escorted out of the building. Sexual assault was common across institutionalized populations at this time (see, for example, Sullivan *et al.*, 1987).

If medical discourses of the late nineteenth century saw the forced confinement and isolation of people with disabilities within institutions, the early twentieth century heralded an equally monstrous turn in the employment of scientific and medical discourse in the care of disabled and institutionalized

Introduction 7

persons. Out of earlier ambivalent Victorian philosophy, which sought both to educate and to control persons with disabilities, grew the eugenics movement, which endeavoured to 'improve' society's genetic stock through limiting the reproductive capabilities of people deemed socially undesirable. For example, public opinion feared that the 'feeble-minded' would overpopulate, preventing progress to a utopian nation: "[n]o political machinery can prevent an aggregate of degenerate citizens from being a degenerate nation" (Inge, 1909, p. 26). As such, a growing objective of long-term institutionalization was to control the proliferation of those diagnosed as 'feeble-minded' or 'mentally deficient' (Park & Radford, 1998), two terms that extended to the 'morally enfeebled' and the 'incurable,' meaning people who had "heritable intellectual disabilities" (p. 318). Throughout the twentieth century, the Canadian public believed that the number of people with genetic abnormalities threatened to exceed the number of people with 'good' genetic stock, and thus public debate regarding the use of mandatory sterilization policies as a form of protection rather than a means of punishment arose (Dyck, 2013; Park & Radford, 1998). Sterilization programs existed under provincial law in Alberta (1928–1972) and British Columbia (1933–1973).

While Ontario managed to escape the grip of legally sanctioned eugenics policies, the social power of the eugenics movement impacted the institutional climate. Chupik and Wright (2006) note that this rise in "eugenic-inspired ideology … validated the institution and promoted (not always successfully) radical options to protect society from the 'taint' of 'feeble-mindedness'" (p. 78). For example, across Ontario male and female children identified as 'feeble-minded' were placed in gender-specific schools and shelters and older adolescents and adults were sent to Orillia's Hospital School (formerly the Orillia Asylum for Idiots and later the Huronia Regional Centre) for permanent isolation, "before they became a eugenic threat" (Park, 1990, p. 99). Hospital School residents were segregated by gender to limit sexual contact and the possibility of procreation while common medical and public belief in the fecundity of 'feeble-minded' women, and the threat of heritable conditions of disability, meant that females were institutionalized for longer periods than males, often permanently (Park, 1990). In fact, in 1913 Ontario passed the *Act Respecting Houses of Refuge for Females*, which, in the event of a diagnosis of 'feeble-mindedness,' restricted women's rights to be discharged from custodial care (Simmons, 1982, p. 77). Park (1990) writes: "the release of women who were of feeble mind was considered by some influential reformers as not only a crime against Ontario but against the nation" (p. 136).

Against the growth of the eugenics movement, the global experience of World War II resulted in ideological reforms as egalitarian notions developed in response to Nazism (even if, despite public backlash regarding the parallels between west coast and German eugenics, Canadian sterilization programs would not be repealed until the 1970s; see Dyck, 2013). At the same time, the fiscal strain of institutions on the welfare state furthered the perceived need for changes to large, state-funded systems of care

8 *Introduction*

(Mechanic & Rochefort, 1990). Dominant views regarding the treatment of people with intellectual disability were shifting toward community placement and greater independence, away from reliance on total institutions (see Abbas & Voronka, 2014). The community placement system was developed in the United States and introduced in Ontario in 1927 to reduce the costs of care and training but required the establishment of community agencies for public assistance and supervision. However, given the very entrenched social belief in custodial care and the lingering myth of the menace of the feeble-minded (Simmons, 1982), the push toward deinstitutionalization did not gain traction until much later in the century.

The Huronia Regional Centre

Much of this book relies on information gained from the specific study of the Huronia Regional Centre: a total institution for people with developmental disabilities in Orillia, Ontario. Huronia is an important case study in institutional violence for two reasons. First, for much of its tenure, it was the largest facility of its type in Canada, and therefore served as a model for institutional care across the country, and thus may stand in as an exemplar for institutional care across Canada. Second, Huronia was the subject of a landmark class action lawsuit launched by survivors against the Ontario government. This lawsuit was settled out of court in 2013, and opened the door for subsequent class action lawsuits launched against provincial governments for their negligence in managing residential facilities. This book uses documentation from this lawsuit and related case law as well as in-depth ethnographic data collected with and from Huronia survivors. As such, it is important to provide a detailed account of the rise and fall of the Huronia Regional Centre, which serves as an exemplar for many other institutions and institutional practices.

In 1839, the provincial government of Ontario authorized the establishment of the first asylums under the *Act to authorize the erection of an Asylum within this Province for the reception of Insane and Lunatic persons.* In 1857, the government of Ontario used a refurbished hotel in Orillia as a branch of the Toronto asylum and called it the "Convalescent Lunatic Asylum" (Williston, 1971). In 1870 the asylum suffered a gross loss of revenue and closed with the remaining patients transferred to London Ontario's "Idiot Branch" (later to become the Southwestern Regional Centre) in 1873 (Broderick, 2011; Park & Radford, 1998). In response to overcrowding and growing demographic pressures, a new site, then called the "Orillia Asylum for Idiots," opened its doors in 1876 under the guidance of superintendent Dr. Wallace, who believed that care for 'idiots' (people with intellectual disability) demanded more space, seclusion, and social removal than 'lunatics' (people with psychiatric disability). Given the increasing demand for institutional care, the Orillia Asylum expanded from 175 acres in 1880 to 456 acres by 1911 (Park, 1990).

Dr. Helen MacMurchy, Inspector of the Feebleminded from 1906 to 1916, and others believed that temporary homes and training schools were being overrun by mental defectives, and therefore made repeated attempts to transfer

Introduction 9

students to Orillia based on the current standards of intelligence testing. Consequently, the Orillia Asylum was chronically overcrowded with residents who had been removed from the educational system (Chupik & Wright, 2006) and elsewhere. Thus, a small majority of those admitted to the Orillia Asylum came directly from home while most came from a variety of welfare institutions, including the Children's Aid Society, Toronto General Hospital Mental Hygiene Clinic, and various orphanages (Chupik & Wright, 2006). While the asylum housed people of all ages, during the first decade of the twentieth century, the average age of individuals committed to Orillia began to decrease. Administrators established a minimum age of admission of six years old, a policy that was broken only in rare circumstances (Chupik & Wright, 2006).

Rather than defining itself as a catchall institution, the Orillia Asylum's emergent aims were to provide care and treatment for children and adolescents rather than full grown or elderly people (Park, 1990). Park asserts that this shift reflected a growing belief in early detection and intervention as a means to "control feeblemindedness" (p. 98). This may also be in part due to the fact that other social service providers, such as the Children's Aid Society, turned to the Orillia Asylum as both a last resort for very difficult children, and a secure housing option when children became too old for public assistance (often around age 12). As Chupik and Wright (2006) describe: "a diagnosis of 'mental defectiveness' and admission to Orillia ... would secure permanent public funds for these older children" (p. 83). Asylum staff actively discouraged parents from visiting, and the asylum's geographical seclusion meant that patients were extremely isolated, and even regular interaction with families was made very difficult, if not impossible (Park, 1990).

Despite stated aims, Simmons (1982) notes that Orillia was a "jumble" and "always much more than the hospital and training school it claimed to be" (p. 134) and therefore housed a much wider variety of people with a far greater range of disability and need than could be supported by the limited resources provided. For example, in the 1930s, "Orillia ... [housed] a certain number of senile old, severely retarded, multiply handicapped, or syphilitic people – those who for physical and mental reason would not survive outside an institution," (p. 134) as well as an assortment of people who were not disabled but simply required social welfare, including orphans, teenage mothers, and "indigents" (p. 134). Regardless of the route, the Orillia Asylum was populated with children and adults for whom the isolated facility became a life-long place of residence.

The Orillia Asylum, renamed the Orillia Hospital School in the early twentieth century,[1] was built to impress the public from afar, and suggested a level of grandeur and elegance. From outside the gates of Orillia, the property boasted a long driveway leading to a magnificent-looking château built in the countryside along the shores of Lake Simcoe, where medical experts believed that patients would benefit from constant contact with fresh air and pastoral farmland settings, as well as social and geographical isolation. But, in reality, the Orillia Asylum was overcrowded and underfunded, particularly in comparison to facilities which housed mentally ill patients (Park, 1990) and facilities abroad.

10 Introduction

Figure 1.1 This undated postcard shows a bucolic image of the Orillia Asylum for Idiots (later renamed the Huronia Regional Centre) in its infancy.

In fact, Simmons (1982) notes that the per patient cost of care at Orillia at the start of the twentieth century was among the lowest in the world – in some cases, less than half of what was paid per patient at similar institutions in the United States. Simmons explains that these dramatic differences in cost reflected a reliance on in-house labour (i.e., using patient labour to support the facility) and a chronically small and underpaid staff complement. Indeed, the average monthly wage for an Orillia staff person was $29.32 CAD, while his or her American counterpart earned $73.82, and the staff-to-patient ratio was 1:14 versus 1:7 at US asylums. Even at this time, officials noted that these cost containment strategies negatively impacted the level of care provided at Orillia. Provincial inspector O'Reilly noted that American caregivers were superior to those in Ontario and "the asylums were furnished more expensively with more money spent on books, periodicals, newspaper and amusements" (Simmons, 1982, p. 33). Further, care for the facility was shared by the Department of Public Works, which maintained responsibility for determining the size, location, design, construction of the site, and the Department of Health, which oversaw the management of the Hospital School in terms of staff and resources. However, there was little coordination between the two departments and necessary changes and upgrades were slow and poorly planned (Berton, 1960; Williston, 1971).

The putative health and therapeutic benefits of rural isolation and vocational training (see Park, 1990) provided ample justification for the instatement of onsite farming and other forms of unpaid labour as a practice at Orillia. As of 1880, farm colonies for people with intellectual disability became accepted

Introduction 11

medical-administrative practice, and "the belief became prevalent that with enough land, an institution could become self-supporting" (Williston, 1971, p. 23). This practice was doubly beneficial to administrators: it kept patients occupied and reduced the need for staff. Unpaid residents completed the laundry and kitchen tasks, general household duties, and manual labour. Thus, perpetual gross underfunding undermined any benevolent intentions and placed the health and welfare of residents in jeopardy. Park (1990) notes that, by 1931, the conditions at Huronia were impoverished and unsanitary (p. 46). At institutions like Orillia's Hospital School, chronic understaffing became the norm, as 'higher grade' patients cared for 'lower grade' patients, performed cleaning and maintenance duties, and produced food for the institution, all without remuneration. Williston (1971) notes that "those capable of being absorbed into society constituted a major labour force for the institution and were too valuable to be released" (p. 24). Administrators of Orillia's Hospital School reiterated the importance of isolating people with disabilities, noting that, "families should release their children to us and not interfere with our management" (Williston, 1971, p. 29).

Public concern regarding the institution was first piqued when a female patient's death at Orillia's Hospital School became publicized. A fire broke out, and the supervising nurse was called to help evacuate the main building, leaving patients alone in the infirmary. Unable to evacuate by herself, the female patient suffocated and died (Berton, 1960). Responding to this type of incident, and demonstrating their growing mistrust of institutionalized care, Canadian citizens began to organize with local and provincial associations, lobbying the government to coordinate advocacy efforts across Ontario. This growing lobby resulted in the birth of the Ontario Association for Retarded Children in 1958, now the Canadian Association for Community Living (Caplan, 1991). Medical and political propaganda of the 1960s pushed back against these efforts and maintained that "three of every 200 children born in Ontario would require institutional care" (Gutnick, 2011). Given the lack of community and social support for caring for persons with disabilities at the time, even families who were wary of institutionalization were left with few viable options.

Public opinion further shifted in 1960, when Pierre Berton, a famed *Toronto Star* journalist, made an impromptu visit to Orillia's Hospital School. Following this visit, Berton (1960) published an excoriating article publicizing the horrific conditions of the institution. Upon entering Orillia's Hospital School, Berton found almost 3,000 occupants crowded into facilities that could more reasonably fit 2,000. In his column, he wrote that beds were positioned head to head on the verandas, in the classrooms, and occupying the playroom. The paint was peeling off the walls, there were gaping holes in the floors and plaster, and the roof leaked. "The stench," Berton reported, "[was] appalling, even in winter. Many patients [were] helpless and [could not] use toilets; floors scrubbed three times a day by overworked staff" (1960, para. 1).

Newer 'cottages' (which were, in fact, just outbuildings, and often shoddy) at Orillia's Hospital School, originally designed for integrating 'high grade'

12 Introduction

patients into community life, were being misused and overcrowded, each housing patients with limited mobility because newer 'cottages' were at less risk of catching fire than older, more flammable buildings (Berton, 1960; Williston, 1971). Berton (1960) argued that the underlying problem at Orillia's Hospital School was public and political neglect, writing that it seemed "easier to appropriate funds for spectacular public projects such as highways and airports than for living space for tiny tots with clouded minds" (para. 15). Berton's article caused a public ripple. Over the days following this publication, reporting within the *Toronto Star* verified Berton's claims, and then-Health Minister M. B. Dymond admitted facilities were overcrowded and decrepit ("Orillia Charges 'True,'" 1960). Blame was passed from political hand to political hand, from hospital administrative staff to politicians. Orillia Hospital's superintendent Foster C. Hamilton attributed "at least 30 percent" of the overcrowding to pressure from Members of (Ontario) Provincial Parliament (MPP) to admit individuals, which he called a "political racket" ("Charges MPP Pressure James Mental Hospital," 1960, para. 4). Park (1990) argues that administrative stagnation and short-term policy decisions at the time only marginally changed institutional practices that failed to address or resolve any rapidly compounding problems.

Figure 1.2 An image of a window looking out from Huronia's decrepit "K" cottage, covered in wire caging material. A small sticker on the window reads "no justice, no peace."
Photographer Marilyn Dolmage.

Introduction 13

Following the revelations of Berton and others, and in the face of mounting social pressures to end institutionalization and re-route people with intellectual disabilities into forms of community care, the Huronia Regional Centre gradually de-institutionalized its residents, closing for good in 2009. In 2010, Patricia Seth and Marie Slark, aided by litigation guardians Jim and Marilyn Dolmage, embarked on a legal quest to seek justice and remediation for those who had lived at Huronia between 1945 and 2009. The lawsuit readied itself for trial, but settled out of court in 2013 for 36 million dollars, giving survivors the ability to make individual financial claims for up to $42,000. This lawsuit was important not only for Huronia survivors, but also because it opened the door to a string of related class action lawsuits on behalf of survivors of institutions across Ontario, including the Southwestern Regional Centre, Rideau Regional Centre, and other such Schedule 1 facilities, or facilities that under Ontario law housed persons with intellectual disabilities; as well as schools for blind and deaf children. These cases have provided some sense of justice for people who suffered within institutions, and have provided an enormous amount of information about what it was like to live within such spaces.

Mixed methods, disturbing data

Institutional violence is, we have argued, a pressing yet under-examined social issue. Our work seeks to ameliorate the paucity of empirical and theoretical material about disability and institutional violence through an interdisciplinary approach. We draw from legal studies, disability studies, and critical social and psychological theory in order to provide a working theoretical model of what institutional violence is and how and why it occurs with such regularity. To do so, this work is grounded in the experiences of people who lived through institutional violence, and relies on a wide range of primary data, including oral histories of institutional survivors and staff, ethnographic observation, legal proceedings, and archival data.

Legal analysis

Huronia survivors Marie Slark and Patricia Seth spearheaded a watershed moment in Canadian litigation: a class action civil lawsuit against the government of Ontario for failing in its fiduciary duty in relation to the mistreatment of persons with intellectual disability diagnoses experienced while institutionalized at the Huronia Regional Centre. They first filed their complaint with the help of litigation guardians Marilyn and Jim Dolmage in 2010, on behalf of residents who lived at Huronia from 1945 until the day Huronia shut down in 2009. The class alleged that the Crown failed in its duties to institutional residents, specifically their duties to fund, operate, manage, administer, supervise, and control goings-on at the Huronia Regional Centre. In overseeing this facility, they argued, the state had failed to enact prevention policies or to improve quality of care,

14 *Introduction*

notwithstanding reports of overcrowding and understaffing, and recommendations for improvement. This breach in their duty of care resulted in emotional, physical, and psychological abuse (see *Dolmage v Ontario*, 2010, ONSC 1726, para. 29).

In 2013, the case was settled out of court for, among other gains, a $35 million compensation package, in addition to expenses for administering the claims process, and the promise that compensation awards would not be subject to taxation or claw-backs (*Dolmage v HMQ*, 2013, para. 13). There were also non-monetary benefits, including a formal apology delivered by the Premier of Ontario; the production of archival materials and scholarly research; and commemorative initiatives, including a memorial plaque, a registry for survivors, signage on the Huronia cemetery grounds, scheduled access to the Huronia site, and scholarly opportunities to archive artifacts.

This lawsuit, and its resultant settlement, drew public attention to the experiences of persons with intellectual disability diagnoses in institutional settings, and called upon Ontario's legal system to grapple with locating responsibility and responding to survivors of a collective trauma. There is therapeutic and political value in tort litigation like that pursued by the class of Huronia survivors. Tort is an area in law where private citizens can pursue legal recourse to hold liable, usually but not always in monetary forms, those who have caused them injury. The burden of proof is not as high as that in criminal proceedings, so the processes for evaluating the veracity of claims are not as rigorous. Tort's guiding legal principle is corrective justice, where a tortfeasor or wrongdoer is held to account and expected to compensate the wronged.

The settlement was also important for disability justice because it offered a blueprint for what would come to be called the Institutional Cases. The cases constitute a collection of class action lawsuits launched since 2011 by survivors of institutions across Canada, and especially Schedule 1 facilities in Ontario, like Huronia. The legal materials generated from these challenges and settlements – some ongoing, others resolved – offer a wealth of information on institutionalization, and specifically examples of and conditions for institutional violence. Their entry into public record catalysed political and legal discourse that articulated the legacy of institutions, and that framed institutionalization as a wrong. Our use of legal research methods enables us to piece together narratives regarding shared experiences of injury.

Specifically, legal research methods entail tracing the history of legal principle through statutory law and judicial decisions. Much of the story of Huronia has unfolded in legal materials, as well as policy reports regarding the institution and archival records on residents – documentation entered into evidentiary record of court cases. Accordingly, we are turning to law to flesh out Canada's institutional history and to develop a theory of institutional violence. Typical analysis born of legal research methods engages

Introduction 15

with socio-legal research and more broadly critical theory and social science scholarship to make sense of law's relationship with and role in society. This means we can draw from socio-legal theory to illustrate the potential and the limitations of the class action lawsuits that have largely been at the heart of Huronia's recounting.

Recounting Huronia

Much of the material for this book was collected as part of a long-term research project called *Recounting Huronia*. As the landmark class action made its way toward court, a small group of researchers, allies, and Huronia survivors formed an arts-based research collective in order to collect and preserve important stories of institutionalization and institutional survival disclosed by those involved in the court case. It was clear that the justice system, while important as a means of making public stories of violence, was limited in terms of determining which stories could be told, who got to tell these stories, and how these stories were mediated. The Huronia survivors involved in the court case wanted not only their day in court, but also other means of expressing the horrors of what occurred at Huronia, without the strictures of the legal system impinging on their ability to recount their experiences.

The *Recounting Huronia* research project was funded by the Social Science and Humanities Research Council of Canada (SSHRC) in 2014. Comprised of a total of 24 group members, the group included nine Huronia survivors – four women and five men – five researchers from universities across southern Ontario, three graduate students, and seven allies and community artists. While some of the group members worked on the project for a short time, the majority of the members, including the survivors in the group, remained in the project for the duration – three years in total. All of the survivors in the group were older adults (ranging in age from early fifties to early seventies) who had at some point been labelled by medical and psychiatric professionals both inside and outside the institution as having an intellectual disability. This diagnosis had been revoked later in life (through professionally administered IQ testing) for at least one group member. Many survivor members of the group had multiple diagnoses, including PTSD, depression, and a variety of physical impairments. Each survivor in the group had lived at Huronia for a period of years – even decades – beginning in childhood and early adolescence. All were de-institutionalized in late adolescence or early adulthood. All but two members now live independently; many left the institution to live as productive, working community members. Ethics approval was sought and received from the research ethics boards at all the respective post-secondary institutions involved.

The *Recounting Huronia* project aimed to be both emancipatory and participatory, meaning that decision-making was, as often as possible,

16 *Introduction*

collaborative and flexible. Telling stories about trauma is emotionally fraught; to accommodate this, we moved very slowly through the project, leaving ample time for all group members to get to know one another and to develop rapport and comfort with one another and the process. Because histories of institutional survivors are deeply personal and highly complex, the *Recounting Huronia* project relied both on arts-based ethnographic methodologies, which allow for a high degree of flexibility and openness in regards to narrative expression and analysis (see davis halifax *et al.* 2017), and more traditional forms of data collection such as in-depth interviews.

Ethnography is a research methodology that aims to elucidate and provide interpretation for the "meanings, functions, and consequences of human actions and institutional practices" (Hammersley & Atkinson, 1995, p. 3). The *Recounting Huronia* project, and consequently the material for *Punishing Conditions*, relied heavily on ethnographic practices to collect and make sense of data. The authors of this book spent the three years of the project not only getting to know participants, but also undertaking the ethnographic process of what Geertz calls "deep hanging out," or closely observing the words, actions, interactions and dynamics of the survivor members of the group, and working to make sense of these observations within the context of Huronia's history, artifacts, and the institutional site itself.

Our first collective activity was to spend a weekend visiting the Huronia site. The Huronia campus closed in 2009 and has been essentially abandoned and off limits to the public for several years. As part of the lawsuit's settlement, Ontario's Ministry of Community and Social Services opened the Huronia site for three public visitations, each lasting a weekend. During this time, survivors, family members, former staff, and members of the general public were able to tour the grounds and buildings. The *Recounting Huronia* research team visited the site on the final visitation weekend in October 2014.

On this visit, we broke into research dyads – pairs of survivors and researchers – who worked together to take photographs and videos, and conduct interviews while at the site. Survivor team members led their researcher partners on tours of the site, visiting the spaces in which they had lived and worked, while the researcher team members recorded these tours and used this as an opportunity to ask questions and gain insight into what life was like at Huronia. Importantly, the survivors in the group provided rich narrative detail about the space of the institution itself. For example, survivors described in detail which rooms were used for what kinds of punishment, showed the researchers in the group where they had slept and in what kinds of conditions, where and how they were bathed, where and how they ate, and where they went for medical treatment. Our project members were also given access to a wide variety of institutional artifacts that the survivors in the group were able to contextualize. These included items such as crib cages used for housing highly impaired residents, belts used for whipping, and thermometers used to gauge the proper temperature of a punitive bath.

Figure 1.3 An image of a cage-like "crib cot" used to hold children and adults with severe physical disabilities taken at Huronia following its closure. Crib cots featured bars on all four sides as well on top to prevent residents from climbing out, and thus represent another form of isolation within the institution.
Photographer nancy viva davis halifax.

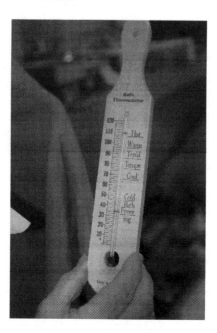

Figure 1.4 An image of a bath thermometer used at the Huronia Regional Centre in order to discern the correct temperature for punitive ice baths.
Photographer nancy viva davis halifax.

18   *Introduction*

During this visit, we also collectively worked to intervene in and on the space in two different ways. We collectively worked with two sound artists, Christof Migone and Marla Hlady, on a sound installation in which survivor-members of the project 'spoke' directly into the walls of the institution (Hlady & Migone, 2017). Their voices, and the stories they chose to tell, were amplified and magnified by industrial speakers attached to the institution's walls. The effect was that the survivors' stories literally shook the institution's foundations and rattled its walls. The group also visited the Huronia cemetery, where thousands of former residents are buried in un-named graves.[2] Many survivors think about those who died in the institution, and the survivor group members felt that it was imperative to visit the cemetery at the end of each day to pay respects and to reaffirm their commitment to this work on behalf of those who did not survive Huronia.

We remained in our research dyads for the rest of the three-year project. Following the site visit, from late 2014 to early 2017, we conducted monthly arts-based workshops designed to elicit experiences about life at Huronia. During these workshops, the team came together as a whole in order to explore some piece of the experience of institutional survival. Together, we used photography, collage, poetry, and theatre to express a variety of stories of institutionalization and survival. For example, using a poetic template created by the researcher team members, the survivor team members used creative language in order to recount their experience of first entering Huronia. Rather than asking direct questions about the process of being admitted and evaluated, we instead focused on using poetry to gain a deeply subjective, expressive, and impressionistic account of survivors' memories of their first days in the institution. Similarly, the survivors used collage and drawing to reflect on difficult parts of their Huronia experience. Ultimately, the team created a cabaret that reflected and showcased much of the arts-based explorations of institutional life. However, these arts-based pieces also comprise an important data set as they articulate details of survivor experience that are beyond language, or impossible to wrestle into a cohesive narrative.

While each survivor worked closely with a researcher or graduate student in the group in order to complete the arts-based pieces, the workshops also functioned as cumulative and unstructured focus groups: the survivors naturally reminisced with one another about their time incarcerated and these discussions unearthed many collective memories about routines, staff, and events at Huronia. The research team members took detailed notes about these workshops/focus groups, linking observations regarding group narratives and dynamics back to the ethnographic observations we made collectively during the site visit weekend. The workshops were also audio and video recorded and the researcher members of the team held regular, lengthy debriefing sessions following each workshop to compare observations and to begin the nascent process of analysis.

Introduction 19

Beyond the arts-based work, which informs our analysis here by providing narrative and observational detail shared by and between survivors, this book also draws heavily on a series of in-depth key informant interviews performed by the authors with seven of the survivor-members of the project. These interviews took place over a series of several months. Each interview lasted about an hour, and survivors were interviewed multiple times. These interviews were conducted on the phone, in survivors' homes, and in public places like restaurants and libraries. Each survivor was eager to tell their story, and embraced the prospect of being interviewed in the hopes that their story would help someone else. The interviews were transcribed and coded using NVIVO qualitative software. Importantly, the goal of these interviews was *not* to ask the survivors to detail experiences of violence, but rather to gain a better understanding about daily living routines in the institution. As such, we asked about eating, sleeping, bathing, and medical routines at Huronia. However, it was impossible for survivors to answer these questions without detailing experiences of profound violence and neglect.

Structure of the book

Institutional Violence and Disability: Punishing Conditions wrestles with the problem of institutionalization through a series of related essay-chapters, each of which theorizes institutional violence from a different perspective. Chapter 2, *The Institutional Cases and the conditions for moral abdication*, sets the stage for the analysis contained in the book in two respects. First, it lays theoretical groundwork that understands institutional violence as situational, and as a problem of *moral abdication*, rather than individual perversion. Second, it provides a broad overview of institutional violence through legal analysis – specifically, the analysis of class action lawsuits called the Institutional Cases, launched in Ontario on behalf of persons with disabilities who purport to have been abused and neglected while in institutional care. These cases are broad ranging and include institutions for people with intellectual disabilities, seeing and hearing impairments, and psychiatric disabilities. The Institutional Cases are important because they provide detailed descriptions of institutional organizational practices, and thus allow us to draw parallels between institutions. Using an analysis of these cases that relies on Albert Bandura's notion of situational moral disengagement, we argue in this chapter that there are several key organizational factors common to many institutions that foster moral abdication and lead to extreme forms of violence.

Chapter 3, *The institutional violence continuum*, focuses on what spaces of moral abdication look like in practice. To do so, we explore the lived experiences of people who were incarcerated at the Huronia Regional Centre. This chapter draws from several oral histories performed with Huronia survivors in order to better understand what institutional violence looked and felt like

20   *Introduction*

on a daily basis. Relying on these narratives, and drawing from sociological theory, particularly sociologist Goffman's work on total institutions, to help identify and taxonomize the kinds of violence inflicted on Huronia residents, this chapter at once describes and categorizes the violence recounted by survivors. This categorization is crucial because it illustrates the ways in which seemingly benign and benevolent forms of institutional care in fact comprise a kind of violence and pave the way for more egregious instances of physical and sexual brutality.

Chapter 4, *Thoughtlessness and violence as work culture*, shores up accounts given by past and present institutional staff and administrators, as well as their relatives, who justify their conduct as care; and draws from political philosophy to treat these accounts to critical analysis. Legal defences and opinion editorials from the perspectives of staff are designed to distance moral actors from violent acts of the institution, and in so doing conceptualize institutional violence as exceptional and radical. The incommensurability of staff perspectives with institutional survivors' testimony calls for a closer reading of how staff may have experienced or understood the violence of which they were a part. We deconstruct narrow and spectacularized conceptualizations of institutional violence using political theorist Hannah Arendt's work, particularly her interest in how totalitarian mentalities fold moral actors into administrative machinery that diffuses responsibility for the violence inflicted. To be a cog in the machinery requires a commitment to thoughtlessness, or a lack of criticality – a phenomenon that has been popularized as the *banality of evil*. We follow through on Arendt's call to resist all impulses to mythologize the horrible in our analysis of institutional violence as a thought-defying milieu. This chapter closes on consideration of the impossibility of using legal instruments to approach evil in its most banal terms, and the problem of demythologizing victim affect.

Chapter 5, *Quantifying and re-inscribing violence*, argues that the violence of the institution does not disappear once institutionalization has ended, but extends beyond de-institutionalization and inflicts itself on institutional survivors in new ways. This chapter returns to legal analysis in order to look at a secondary form of violence experienced by institutional survivors: discursive violence. We argue that, although the class action lawsuits described in our first chapter were an attempt at justice, the result of these lawsuits has been, for many, a re-visitation and re-entrenchment of the kinds of bodily violence they endured while incarcerated. As such we look at the specific wording used by the Crown in the settlement of the Huronia class action lawsuit, which delineated which kinds of survivor accounts of trauma would be remunerated. Here we use discourse analysis to uncover how this particular legal construction of justice forced survivors to not only describe but indeed to quantify their trauma. Central to the settlement is a points system that asks survivors to provide detailed descriptions of their experience of institutional violence, and then assigns a point value for these descriptions, which

Introduction 21

entitles each survivor to an amount of settlement money, depending on how many points they have been awarded for their description. This means that survivors without access to language (i.e., survivors who are non-verbal) or memory (i.e., survivors who have repressed traumatic memory) have been left out of the settlement process and have not received as much financial compensation as verbal survivors who are able to recall and describe their trauma. This, of course, has led to a dangerous hierarchicalization of traumatic experience that pits one survivor's testimony against another's, and leaves those unable to speak or remember – generally the most vulnerable and traumatized – outside the machinations of legal justice.

The final substantive chapter of this book, *Embedded trauma and embodied resistance*, extends the arguments made in Chapter Five but, rather than looking at external loci of institutional re-traumatization, instead examines how the organizational traits that lead to institutional violence are indelibly inscribed in and on survivors' bodies. Here, we think about how organizational structure itself becomes embodied and therefore reproduced and re-performed over a lifetime, regardless of whether one is incarcerated or not. This is to say that institutional practices, especially including violence, become bound up with the embodied economy of institutionalized people: institutional forms become an *embodied way of life: the body reproduces violent institutional forms, and at the same time resists them.* This chapter, which is reflective in nature, draws from impressionistic observations made over the course of the *Recounting Huronia* project, and specifically engages the embodied actions and routines of the survivor-members as a way of making sense of institutional violence as an ongoing embodied practice.

In our concluding chapter, we turn away from total institutions and toward alternate models of care for people with disabilities, or who are otherwise vulnerable. We ask: what possibilities exist to encompass persons who rely on external support while at the same time maintaining the primacy of individual liberty, dignity, and personhood? To do so, we look at three examples of places that provide care without relying on institutional organizational norms, thereby sidestepping the situational routes to violence we have described in earlier chapters. First, we look at the Camphill movement: a worldwide series of intentional communities rooted in the philosophy of Rudolf Steiner, designed to support and incorporate persons with intellectual disabilities into family homes. Second, we look at the L'Arche movement, founded by Jean Vanier, which, like the Camphill movement places people with intellectual disability at the centre of community through intentional living arrangements. Finally, we look at the small town of Geel, Belgium, which has welcomed people with psychiatric disabilities into their midst since the fourteenth century and has provided support through a network of loving foster families and community care. These models bear striking organizational similarities to one another, which, we assert, offer the possibility for care beyond violence.

22   *Introduction*

Notes

1　The exact date of this name change is unclear. Simmons mentions the name being in use as early as 1929, while other sources credit the name change as happening in the early 1930s. The precise date seems to be missing from current records.
2　The Huronia cemetery is a particularly fraught space: many residents were buried under numbered, instead of named, paving stones. These stones were later repurposed for use in a walkway, leaving these residents unmarked in death and further degraded.

2   The Institutional Cases and the conditions for moral abdication

Survivors and allies have made public shocking accounts of institutional violence over the last two decades, and yet there remains a relative paucity of scholarly work that helps explain how caregiving institutions become spaces of profound abuse. Thus, in this chapter we ask: what structural and organizational factors foster an institutional culture in which extreme violence is not only tolerated but normalized and, perhaps most disturbingly, even enjoyed? In other words: how does the organizational structure of such institutions allow, and even nurture, a culture of *moral abdication*? In response, we provide a comparative analysis of the 'Institutional Cases,' a trend in civil litigation seeking to hold provincial governments responsible for horrific violence and neglect endured by former institutional residents.[1] These class action lawsuits provide important insight into not only what kinds of violence many institutionalized people have suffered, but also about common *organizational* practices that we believe lead to profound forms of violence within institutional settings.

In this chapter, we first define the key theoretical perspectives underpinning this analysis, focusing on Banduran theory of *situational moral disengagement* as a means to making sense of institutional violence. Second, we turn to the Institutional Cases to describe situational violence as it unfolded in Canadian institutional settings. Third, we provide a comparative analysis of these examples, and describe five key organizational factors that may influence and nurture moral abandonment and the creation of an ethos of violence.

Theoretical framework

Accounts of institutional abuse are often either rooted in micro-analyses (i.e., individual accounts) of violence, or in very broad structural critiques as a means to understanding how institutional violence has come to pass. Sociologist Carina Heckert asserts that social scientific analyses regarding violence have too often focused on broad structural critiques (i.e., neoliberalism and its social corollaries: systemic poverty, political turmoil, lack of human and physical resources, etc.) as a means to account for widespread but

24 *Institutional Cases and moral abdication*

micro-level forms of institutional violence and neglect (Heckert, 2016). While theories of violence would be remiss for overlooking these broad conditions, they tend to lose track of the agential role perpetrators of violence play, and so lose sight of how to hold perpetrators to account. And yet, individual micro-level analyses too often rely on a dispositional, or 'bad apple,' explanation for how and why violence occurs; that is, that instances of violence are unique outliers perpetrated by disturbed or difficult individuals or groups, thereby missing structural/structuring effects of the wider environment.

'Bad apple' behaviour itself can be understood from a number of perspectives – from individual psychopathy or sociopathy to individual experience of structural or interpersonal violence – but leaves absent a perspective that understands violence as situational, and doesn't explain what kinds of situations 'turn on' or flip the switch for fairly ordinary people to become torturers or sadists. Missing, then, is an analysis that works to understand meso-level factors that influence the creation of *violent milieus.* Relying on forensic individual assessments as the root cause of institutional violence misses the chance to explore the conditioning effects of institutions themselves and to understand organizational dynamics that may lead otherwise ordinary people to become perpetrators of a kind of violence that – in any other setting – would be intolerable and unimaginable. In this work, we offer an analysis of the kinds of organizational factors within institutions that invariably breed deep forms of violence.

Philip Zimbardo (2007), author of *The Lucifer Effect* and architect of the infamous Stanford Prison Experiments, calls individual explanations for violence "dispositional," suggesting they rely on individual dispositions to explain why violence occurs.[2] He instead proposes a *situational* analysis of violence – a theoretical assertion that human beings are capable of extreme forms of violence given the right situation or circumstance, and despite the good intentions of the individual(s) in question. He writes:

> we can assume that most people, most of the time, are moral creatures. But imagine that this morality is like a gearshift that at times gets pushed into neutral. When that happens, morality is disengaged… It is then the nature of the circumstances that determines outcomes, not the driver's skills or intentions.
>
> (p. 17)

Drawing from Milgram's (1974) foundational work, Zimbardo offers a series of social steps for enticing normal people to do things they might otherwise never believe themselves capable of. These include presenting acceptable justification for violence, providing meaningful roles for people to play in which violence is an active part, and creating situations in which responsibility for violence is diffused.

Social psychologist Albert Bandura offers greater nuance, his work moving beyond a situational analysis of violence, or "evil" as Zimbardo terms

Institutional Cases and moral abdication 25

it, toward a more concrete theory of morality, and more specifically moral failing. In basic terms, morality is the adherence to a certain set of socially agreed upon values or principles, which themselves provide the structure for a harmonious social life – that is, harmonious relations between people.[3] Thus, moral codes are often explicit in their prohibition of undue pain or suffering and the maintenance of human dignity. Bandura theorizes a capacity for moral agency, whereby social cognitive development involves adopting and enacting standards of right or wrong that guide self-regulatory behaviour. He conceives of the moral compass as agential to the extent that the subject carries intentionality, forethought, and the capacities to regulate and reflect upon the self; but not as naked free will – a concept he dismisses as a medieval throwback. Rather, the moral subject is socially situated, and thus reacting and contributing to a "reciprocal interplay of intrapersonal, behavioural, and environmental determinants" (Bandura, 2006, p. 165).

This interplay does not always carry the alchemy to produce a moral agent (that is, an agent who is moral). Bandura writes about what he calls "moral disengagement" – moments when moral codes are abandoned (Bandura *et al.*, 1996; Bandura, 2002). Morality, Bandura argues, is not born of dispassionate or abstracted logic, but rather is contextual, and relational. That is to say, morality as an iterative or accumulative practice develops between people, and is contingent on the interplay between people. Bandura writes: "People do not operate as autonomous moral agents, impervious to the social realities in which they are enmeshed. … Self-regulatory mechanisms do not operate unless they are activated" (2002, p. 102). This is to say that morality is neither inherent nor essential. It is not based on a fixed series of innate human qualities, but is fluid and dynamic, shaped by social forces and situations. Perhaps most importantly, it can be completely abandoned in the place of stronger social pressures.

In his model, Bandura (1999) theorizes that moral disengagement occurs through several linked "cognitive mechanisms," or cognitive shifts that allow the denial of moral agency. These cognitive shifts are four-fold. First, one's notion of the inhumane behaviour itself is reconstructed, for example through the use of moral justification, palliative comparisons and euphemistic labelling. For example, abusive punishment within the institution might be recast as behaviour modification, which applies a euphemistic label and a moral justification for violence. Second, one's sense of the deleterious effects of one's conduct might be reconstructed through acts such as minimizing, misconstruing, or ignoring one's own impact. For example, institutional abuse might be overlooked because of a belief that people with disabilities do not feel pain the same way as people without disabilities, or cannot make sense of violence or forget it immediately. Third, one's own responsibility for the impact of one's damaging behaviour or conduct might be shifted or denied. For example, within the institution, abuse might be blamed on a chain of command or on institutional practices, rather than on individual choices to inflict suffering. Fourth, and finally, one's perception of the

26 *Institutional Cases and moral abdication*

subject who has sustained harm might be shifted through dehumanization or victim blaming. For example, institutional abuse rests on widespread beliefs that people with disabilities are not quite human, less than human, or in need of very intense behavioural modification and bodily control because they are 'not like the others.'

Bandura's model is important to this work for three reasons. First, because he locates 'evil' as a problem of morality, and theorizes that morality is mutable and even dispensable. Second, he provides a description of moral agency linked to moral *action* (or inaction) as opposed simply to moral reasoning (1999). Third, he provides a working model for how and when moral disengagement takes place. This model gives us a micro-level analysis that finds moral disengagement in the interactions between individuals and organizations. However, while Bandura's work is very important in terms of locating micro-level (i.e., interpersonal and individual) cognitive shifts that lead to moral disengagement, what he misses are the specific *organizational* traits that create the fertile ground in which these cognitive mechanisms flourish. In other words, it is still necessary to explore what kinds of social organizations actively promote the abandonment of morality. In this book, we also reframe moral disengagement as *moral abdication* or *moral abandonment*, to signal that the turn away from moral self-regulation is an active, not a passive, process.

The Institutional Cases

To make sense of how institutional settings facilitate situational violence, we considered institutions cited and described in case law. Doing so required that we use legal research methods, a scholarly approach that traces the development of legal principle and precedent through common law documents. Legal reports and their supporting documentation yield a wealth of information on legal decision-making but also on social patterns and the development of collectively held values, to the extent that legal and social institutions share a complex, co-constitutive relationship (Luhmann, 1985, 1989). For our analysis, we draw upon class action lawsuits, or civil litigation brought by representatives of a class of persons who share common injuries from a common perpetrator. The class actions of relevance involve classes of persons who had previously been residents, or family members of residents, of institutions designed to hold and care for persons diagnosed with various disabilities. The class actions in question (with one exception) were brought against the government of Ontario for funding, operation, management, administration, supervision, and control of institutions that served as settings for physical and sexual abuse.

Dubbed the Institutional Cases, a string of lawsuits of this nature laid bare (through outlining respective material facts) the extremely violent conditions residents experienced while institutionalized. Through legal research methods, we can discern clear patterns not only of common examples

Institutional Cases and moral abdication   27

of harm, but also of the institutions' common conditions that structured and made possible the violence residents experienced. In case law we find a concentration of ignored reports on conditions of care, survivor accounts of abuse, analysis of the state conditions operating at the macro level, and state defences. In short, we find a constellation of differently positioned resources that offer the clearest picture yet of what life was like within institutional walls. The picture painted is elevated through courtroom scrutiny and public documentation, and given credence through court justices' censure of state inaction. The Institutional Cases mark a new chapter in the era of deinstitutionalization, for they mark a reckoning with a long history of abuse, a calling to account of those responsible. Throughout, the case law conveys that there has been a host of moral agents – not just a few 'bad apples,' as evidenced by the sheer volume of case load and the nature of the wrongdoing alleged – situated at different levels of power making the violence in institutionalized settings possible; and not only possible, but pervasive.

Marie Slark and Patricia Seth spearheaded the first of the Institutional Cases by acting as lead plaintiffs for a class of former Huronia Regional Centre residents.[4] Located in Orillia, Ontario, Huronia managed the day-to-day living of persons diagnosed with intellectual disabilities. The class action reached a settlement agreement in 2013, which included a $35-million settlement package, as well as non-monetary damages (*Dolmage v HMQ*, 2013). The *Slark* settlement served as a model for two concurrent suits involving institutions for persons with intellectual disabilities: one brought by David McKillop on behalf of residents of the Rideau Regional Centre in Smith Falls, the other brought by Mary Ellen Fox on behalf of residents of the Southwestern Regional Centre in Blenheim (*Dolmage, McKillop and Bechard v HMQ*, 2014). When Marlene McIntyre brought a class action suit against Ontario for harm suffered at the Adult Occupational Centre in the town of Edgar (the institution is referred to as Edgar in case proceedings), the settlement reached – again modelled after *Slark* – came to encompass an omnibus action on behalf of 12 comparable Schedule 1 facilities (or institutions under the purview of Ontario law that housed persons with diagnoses of intellectual disability).[5] In what was called in court the fifth Institutional Case of its series, class representative Robert Seed settled with the state for the abuse residents endured at the W. Ross MacDonald School for the Blind, located in Brantford (*Seed v Ontario*, 2017). In a lawsuit that remains active (which means that no settlement has yet been reached as of our writing of this chapter), Christopher Welsh is suing the state for the abuse he and his class endured at the Ernest C. Drury School for the Deaf in Milton, the Sir James Whitney School for the Deaf in Bellville, and the Robarts School for the Deaf in London (and at class certification the presiding justice compared the case to *Seed* and *Dolmage*). In what is also an active case, James Templin is suing for treatment endured at the Children's Psychiatric Research Institute in London (*Welsh v Ontario*, 2016; *Templin v HMQ*, 2016).

28 *Institutional Cases and moral abdication*

Though not formally referred to as an Institutional Case, the class action lawsuit brought against attending medical professionals of the Penetanguishene Mental Health Centre (referred to as Oak Ridge) will be included in this analysis (see *Barker v Barker*, 2017).[6] *Barker* admittedly does not easily fit the Institutional Case pattern: the original claim precedes the *Slark* settlement; the action was not brought against the state, but against staff; and its summary judgment does not follow the *Slark* settlement pattern. Nevertheless, developments in *Barker*, emerging in 2017, owe some credit to the turning of the tide in socio-legal approaches to institutionalization, as marked by *Slark*. Further, *Barker* provides a clear and detailed account of institutional conditions that match and extend findings from the previously cited litigation. Finally, contending with *Barker* expands our analysis of disability – so far, encompassing intellectual and physical aspects of disability – to include psychiatric conditions in a fulsome way.[7] Persons with psychiatric disabilities continue to find themselves subjected to institutional conditions, typically in prisons and forensic and medical facilities, so we would be remiss to bracket this population out of our study.[8]

Across this legal history, plaintiffs detail experiences of profound violence. Commonalities include hitting, punching, slapping, and kicking of residents; throwing objects at residents; sneaking up on residents to attack them from behind; the use of restrictive devices, solitary confinement, and medication; sexual assaults, harassment, and forced nudity; starvation and forced feeding; verbal abuse and humiliation. Staff administered curative treatments without consent, despite the physical pain and humiliation involved, and without scientific evidence of effectiveness. Survivors cite the physical injuries produced, their experience of fear and terror, and the trauma sustained following their release. The experiences of violence bear striking resemblances across institutions – across geographic regions, time-periods, and disability populations. As claimed in *Seed*, "the claims advanced [across the Institutional Cases] are systemic and are anchored in the manner in which [the institution] was maintained, administered, without differentiation between each student's [and resident's, and patient's] experience" (*Seed v Ontario*, 2012, para. 142).

Organizational traits that lead to moral abandonment

1. Does the institution understand its inherent function as one of controlling, reforming, or refashioning its residents?

Bandura provides an important set of cognitive mechanisms that allow for moral abdication to occur, and yet these mechanisms miss the superseding *structural* elements of an institution that trigger these mechanisms. If we are to understand how moral abdication occurs within institutions, it is imperative that we understand the key organizational factors that allow moral abdication. We have used Bandura's schematic in order to rate institutions

Institutional Cases and moral abdication   29

according to how likely moral abdication – and therefore violence – is to occur. At baseline, this schematic works to develop a framework for identifying the potential for an institution to redefine, and dehumanize, the incarcerated *human subject* into an *institutional object*. This transformation is key to allowing the kinds of cognitive shifts central to moral abandonment, as described by Bandura.

First, it is important to understand the institution's view of itself in relation to its residents. *Does the institution understand its inherent function as one of controlling, reforming, or refashioning its residents?* Is the stated mandate of the institution one that directly impinges on the subjecthood of those in its grasp? We might also ask this question in the following way: what is the institution's utopian vision of itself and its residents? This question helps us to understand the overall orientation of the institution to its own work. This is important because it helps us to think about the institution's understanding of its own operations of power as it relates to its residents.

Accounts of staff/resident relationships borne out in the case files overwhelmingly identify punitive measures. The affidavits and cross-examinations invoked during the *Slark* proceedings refer to staff actions as motivated by punishment, for example Seth citing being held down in cold water for refusing to eat (*Dolmage v Ontario*, 2010, ONSC 1726, para. 34). In the statement of claim that launched *Bechard*, Fox indicates she understood use of electric shock via a "'cattle-prod' like device" and "time-outs" in small windowless rooms (otherwise known as solitary confinement) as disciplinary measures (*Bechard v Ontario* Statement of Claim, 2010, paras. 16, 27). In the statement of claim that resulted in a settlement involving the 12 Schedule 1 facilities, McIntyre associates the continuous abuse endured at Edgar – manifest as beatings and humiliation – with punishment, for reasons residents found arbitrary or opaque (*McIntyre v Ontario* Statement of Claim, 2014, para. 21). In a recurrent, throbbing theme across the Institutional Cases, these examples abound, describing violence dressed as discipline – carried out in reaction to behaviour that staff sought to correct or realign. Often this behaviour concerned deviations from expected eating and sleeping schedules; that is, disruption of day-to-day processes managed by institutional staff.

Actions designed to control resident behaviour, and to reform or refashion those institutionalized to the point of compliance, carried from residential to educational spaces, as was evident in facilities explicitly organized to operate as schools for students with sensory impairments. The *Seed* proceedings illustrate how visually impaired students experienced abuse in W. Ross MacDonald classrooms, for example having heavy objects thrown at them for not paying attention; alongside the "house parents" who oversaw resident quarters force-feeding students during mealtimes for students who did not finish their food or eat fast enough, and inflicting physical abuse and humiliation on those who left or wet their beds at night (*Seed v Ontario*, 2012, paras. 19–21). Quoted in the case files, Welsh recounts hearing impaired students being slapped in the mouth for making mistakes when

30   *Institutional Cases and moral abdication*

speaking orally, having their arms physically restrained in reaction to their use of sign language, and being forced to wear hearing aids even when they caused pain; alongside punishments for not eating, not staying in bed at night, and wetting the bed (*Welsh v Ontario*, 2016, paras. 23, 26, 33). These examples, where punishment was used to produce compliance in classroom and residential settings alike, demonstrate how violence was meant to be instructive – to modify or redirect behaviour.

In addition to former residents' interpretations of the motivations driving staff treatment, case records also include defences, explanations, and justifications offered by those who inflicted violence. Analysis of these perspectives reinforces and extends our characterization of the instrumental functions of institutional violence. In *Barker*, the physicians responsible for experimental treatments now described as torture did not dispute allegations regarding the nature of treatments, only "whether the programs developed for the Social Therapy Unit at Oak Ridge were beneficial mental health care" (*Barker v Barker*, 2017, para. 32). Attending medical staff presumed the programs – involving nudity, solitary confinement, restraints, verbal confrontation, heavy sedation, and other physically taxing and humiliating techniques – would induce self-discovery and responsibility for poor behaviour (para. 35).[9] An Ontario Ombudsman report on Oak Ridge experiments (written by a commission that included Dr. Barker, and cited in the *Barker* suit) identified net positives to the program: "a very valuable learning experience in self-control and in group support. All members are continually helping each other to find other ways of behaving or living with their uncomfortable feelings more successfully" (para. 47).[10] The removal of clothing, which featured prominently in Oak Ridge programs, medical staff justified as a means of prodding patients to uncover "the private parts of one's mind," coupled with fear that clothing "might be used in a dangerous manner" (para. 50). We might conclude from this collection of examples that violence was a tool used both as punishment (to produce compliant behaviour for the sake of smooth daily facility operation) and as therapy (to produce compliant behaviour indicative of cure) – both of which are reformative ends.

If those administering and staffing an institution understand their goals to be reforming, refashioning, or controlling its residents, their work from the outset has to do with imposing a normative vision of who residents are supposed to be and how they are to behave, and, crucially, that residents are not capable of managing their own formation or development. Therefore, institutional goals of reformation, refashioning, or control indicate a particular orientation: disciplinary intervention, rather than, for example, autonomy or dignity. The instrumentalization of conduct stands in for moral grounds, and circumvents the activation of moral consideration. Institutional conditions reorganize and reconstruct staff responsibilities to residents – to modify residents, to make them better citizens – and as long as this justification and prioritization holds, staff sidestep their responsibility to treat residents as persons.

Institutional Cases and moral abdication 31

2. Does the institution operate under an efficiency or austerity model?

The second important question to ask about institutional conditions is: *does the institution operate under an efficiency or austerity model?* Otherwise stated: in what way does the institution use deprivation or austerity as a guiding principal for its operations? Importantly, this may or may not have any relation to the institution's financial well-being, but rather has to do with an organizational orientation that privileges efficiency, deprivation, and austerity as a means of operating. Understanding institutional resources, real or perceived, is important in three ways. First, it may provide a clue regarding the general social valuation of the institution's residents. Some institutions are, indeed, cash strapped. And, very simply, if social resources are not directed at an institution, this is an indication of how much or little its residents mean within the greater scope of society. Second, a lack of resources leads to the increased need for vertical power structures in order to efficiently manage human resources, necessarily requires a reliance on a smaller number of staff than might be necessary, and leads to the kind of austerity measures that further signal the devaluation of the institution's residents. Again, lack of institutional resources here both emerges from, and redoubles, the sense of the institution's residents as less worthy than others. Third, conditions of austerity lead to a kind of overall experience of deprivation and devaluation. Residents may be forced to work for little or no remuneration, food may be cheap and disgusting, clothing may be ill-fitting and embarrassing.

All the Institutional Cases involving Schedule 1 facilities rest allegations of negligence in part on the state's failure to heed details in Walton B. Williston's 1971 Report on Ontario institutions. The report documents institutional conditions such as substandard staff to patient ratios due to staff and resource shortages, overcrowded facilities, and antiquated buildings (e.g., *Dolmage v Ontario*, 2010, ONSC 1726, para. 15). Also cited in the Institutional Cases, the 1973 Welch Report speaks to Schedule 1 facility residents needing additional special treatment they were not receiving: "The Welch Report determined that, not only did [residents] not receive the level of appropriate care required, but that since the 1960s, there had been little overall improvement in the actual pattern of care received" (*McIntyre v Ontario* Statement of Claim, 2014, para. 17; see also Welch, 1973). Notwithstanding these reports, provincial facilities did not have funding increased, did not develop oversight to prevent staff abuse, and did not improve quality of care (*McIntyre v Ontario* Statement of Claim, 2014, para. 18). Residents felt the impacts of imposed austerity measures. Having to sleep in densely populated open dormitories was commonly featured across litigants' statements of claim. McKillop and Fox respectively recounted having to wear issued shoes and clothing that did not fit their bodies (*McKillop v Ontario* Statement of Claim, 2010, para. 26; *Bechard v Ontario* Statement

32   *Institutional Cases and moral abdication*

of Claim, 2010, para. 26). Highlighted in *Seed*, residential schools for youth with sensory impairments hired unqualified staff who "did not know how to work with students with [disabilities] and saw their job more as caretakers" (*Seed v Ontario*, 2012, para. 18).

Residents themselves became a free pool of labour on which the institution relied. Common across all the case laws was residents' unpaid work related to the upkeep of the institution. For example, at Rideau, McKillop washed dishes and floors, and cared for other residents without pay; and Fox worked in Southwestern's laundry department without pay (*McKillop v Ontario* Statement of Claim, 2010, para. 30; *Bechard v Ontario* Statement of Claim, 2010, para. 30). When reporting on Schedule 1 facilities, Williston observed that "the emphasis of institutionalization was custody, and not training and rehabilitation," suggesting that the custodial model employed was bare-bones, or austere (*McIntyre v Ontario* Statement of Claim, 2014, para. 16). Any skills development was directed toward maintaining the institutions themselves. Institutional administrators consciously and deliberately used unremunerated patient labour and easily justified it as a form of vocational training.

Returning to Bandura's work, discourses calling for a self-sufficiently run institution rationalize insufficient resource provision and alter and normalize punitive modes of austerity. These discourses rewrite substandard meals and clothing as positive modes of cost containment; forced, unremunerated labour as vocational training. *Thus, these discourses rewrite neglect and subjugation as care.* These are cognitive shifts that facilitate moral abdication, to the extent that an austerity operational model minimizes and ignores impacts on residents. The prioritization of efficiency in institutional spaces produces in staff and state an abandonment of responsibilities around recognizing and refraining from violence.

3. Is the institution socially and physically isolated?

The third question from Bandura's adapted model has to do with the institution's social and physical proximity to broader society. *Is the institution socially and physically isolated?* What is its relationship to the wider society, socially and physically? Where is it located? How much contact do residents have with the rest of society? Understanding how institutions are geographically situated is an important indicator of social location and valuation of the resident population. Many institutions are intentionally located quite literally at the margins of society. They are built away from other communities, and may be separated by geography (i.e., located in a rural setting without easy access to an urban centre) or by architecture (i.e., walls, fences, locked wards) or both. The message here, though, is that the institutionalized population needs to be hidden – either because it is a threat to society, or because society is not manageable for the incarcerated group. Regardless, the placement of institutions outside the boundaries of everyday civilization marks the institutionalized population as different, and beyond the bounds of normalcy. This is, then, a marker of dehumanization.

Physical isolation is a recurring feature across Ontarian institutions now known for violent treatment of residents. As the Crown indicates across its statements of defence: "like many jurisdictions, Ontario's early history of developmental services was based in part, on the notion that individuals with developmental disabilities were often best served by segregating them from the rest of the community" (*Dolmage v Ontario* Statement of Defence, 2011, para. 4).[11] The Crown was defending, firstly, the custodial practice of building facilities to warehouse disabled populations – where they would sleep, eat, go to school, and receive care in a concentrated space rather than in community; and, secondly, the regional isolation of institutions themselves located in small towns or on the outskirts of towns. Such practice was common for blind and deaf populations as well: Seed indicates he had to attend W. Ross MacDonald due to a dearth in options for visually impaired persons: "at the time, it was the only educational institution he could attend given his visual impairment. The local school board would not accept him as a student because they could not accommodate him" (*Seed v Ontario*, 2012, para. 15).

Isolation was not only physical. As the Williston Report makes clear, the geographic remoteness of Schedule 1 facilities "caused a dearth of highly trained individuals prepared to relocate" (cited in *McKillop v Ontario* Statement of Claim, 2010, para. 18), meaning regional isolation impacted the number of qualified physicians, psychiatrists, psychologists, nurses, and social workers available to staff these facilities. Further, residents were isolated from their families and communities due to physical distance and strict policy, as indicated in McKillop's statement of claim: "admission procedures contained no opportunity for pre-admission visits and communication between residents and family members were made difficult if not impossible" (*McKillop v. Ontario* Statement of Claim, para. 37). Residential schools for blind and deaf students engendered social isolation through policy as well, by forbidding interaction and restricting communication with people outside the school: "when a child went to Ross MacDonald there was the inside world and the outside world" (*Seed v Ontario*, 2012, paras. 53–54; see also *Welsh v Ontario*, 2016).

Understaffing and under-qualified staff resulted in a nuanced isolation, felt in dorm spaces themselves, when residents experienced abuse at the hands of one another without caregiver intervention. Seed describes how "house parents" responsible for students outside school hours were deliberate in their failures to intervene when students committed acts of sexual abuse, because "it was 'survival of the fittest'" (*Seed v Ontario*, 2012, para. 31). The Oak Ridge experiments also created conditions of profound personal isolation, via imposed solitary confinement, restrained movement, and sensory deprivation. Central to the Capsule Program was a "specially constructed, soundproof, windowless, but continuously lighted room, eight

34 *Institutional Cases and moral abdication*

feet by ten feet in size, furnished only with a soft rug over a foam floor" and an open toilet and wash basin (*Barker v. Barker*, 2017, para. 49). Up to seven patients would populate that room at any one time – fed via straws in the walls, and left to their treatment without cessation for days. These examples of deliberate isolation, with punitive or therapeutic intent, required custodial and medical personnel to morally abandon their charges – that is, a personal abdication of responsibility for their charges. Such abdication works as a prominent condition of possibility for abuse.

In relation to the Banduran (2006) model, when isolation is cemented as institutional practice, this kind of violence becomes less shocking and the detrimental impact of violence becomes obscure. Isolation operates as one of "various psychosocial mechanisms [that] can be used to disengage moral self-sanctions" (p. 171) because it provides an opportunity for administrators and staff to get away with daily incursions and abuses that would not be tolerated in a more open and public system. Because there is little threat of the outside world calling attention to these incursions and abuses, it is easier for cultures of abuse to form within institutions, each culture making its own social codes and routines that are not disrupted by outside influences. In this way, the self-regulating behaviours common to the public sphere are recalibrated.

4. Are the residents of the institution despised, mistrusted, or dehumanized?

Fourth, in order to assess the potential for moral abdication to occur within institutions, we must assess the social position of the incarcerated population. *Are the residents of the institution despised, mistrusted, or dehumanized?* In other words, is the incarcerated population there because they are deemed a threat to, or unfit for, wider society? Institutional staff members' feeling that those they are in charge of are, from the outset, socially undesirable reduces their willingness to acknowledge and act upon a basic, shared sense of humanity, and increases the possibilities for acting from an understanding of the incarcerated population as dehumanized and therefore deserving of violence. Indeed, disabled persons have been the object of social dehumanization for centuries, and have been widely portrayed and perceived as being not whole, damaged, lacking social value and worth, terrifying, bestial, foolish, and damaged. The very act of institutionalization itself indicates a certain level of dehumanization from the outset, as residents are perceived as being incapable of living in 'normal' (i.e. non-disabled) society.

Related to this are the ways in which resident bodies are controlled within the institution, by both the daily institutional routines and by staff themselves. Do residents lack freedom to make choices about their bodily comportment and body routines (what to eat and wear, when to sleep, when to wash, etc.), and do staff have unfettered access to, and control over, the bodies of those incarcerated? The control of bodily comportment both signifies

Institutional Cases and moral abdication   35

and further reiterates dehumanization in an institutionalized populace, as these practices of control rob residents of basic markers of humanization: agency, dignity, control, and choice. Rather, further robbing an already-despised population of basic forms of bodily agency increases staff members' ability to see residents as less than human, and as expendable objects. Bandura (2002) writes: "once dehumanized, [residents] are no longer viewed as persons with feelings, hopes, and concerns but as sub-human objects. They are portrayed as mindless 'savages'... and other despicable wretches" (p. 109). This, Bandura argues, opens the door for violence: "the process of dehumanization is an essential ingredient in the perpetration of inhumanities" (Bandura, 2002, p. 109).

This pattern is clear across the Institutional Cases: residents in all cases were indeed openly mistrusted and sometimes reviled for their disability and, in turn, lacked control over their lives and bodies. In the first statement of defence given in the string of Institutional Cases, the Crown claimed it was impossible to offer choice and opportunity at Huronia Regional Centre (a claim they would continue to make in statements of defence that would follow from the *Dolmage* settlement) when some populations were simply "too disabled to exercise any significant degree of control over their day-to-day lives" (*Dolmage v Ontario* Statement of Defence, 2011, para. 21). The net result, as attested by both McKillop and Fox, was that every aspect of residents' lives was dictated and controlled, the environments at Rideau and Southwestern were prison-like, and day-to-day opportunities and choices were extremely limited (*McKillop v Ontario* Statement of Claim, 2010, para. 15; *Bechard v Ontario* Statement of Claim, 2010, para. 15). Examples include crowded open dorm rooms, and common bathrooms without shower doors (*McKillop v Ontario* Statement of Claim, 2010, para. 25; *Bechard v Ontario* Statement of Claim, 2010, para. 26). Welsh indicates deaf students were "under the Crown's exclusive control and care ... at the mercy of the adults that cared for them" (*Welsh v Ontario* Statement of Claim, 2016, para. 18). The statement of claim filed for *Barker* describes an "atmosphere of coercion and duress inherent in being confined to an institution in what was called 'coercive milieu therapy'" to explain how patients underwent incredibly violent treatment without giving consent (cited in *Eggleston v Barker*, 2003, para. 8). *Barker* marks a dividing line to justify coercive treatment, based on patient capacity: "in situations where patients are quite properly being held against their will until they change it seems humane and helpful to use force, at least to the point of increasing their range of choice" (*Barker v. Barker*, 2017, para. 51).

A Williston Report observation cited across Schedule 1 facility lawsuits suggests that "the Ontario Hospital School system was divorced from mainstream health education and social/family services and could not therefore adequately establish and administer services" (cited in *McKillop v Ontario* Statement of Claim, 2010, para. 18). While this schism was in part due to austerity policy and conditions of isolation, it also speaks to

36 *Institutional Cases and moral abdication*

attitudes about intellectually disabled populations' capacity. McKillop highlights an effect of growing up in the hospital school system: he received "virtually no education at all while at Rideau," learning the same lessons each academic year (*McKillop v Ontario* Statement of Claim, 2010, para. 29). When suing the government for treatment endured at W. Ross MacDonald, Seed describes his own education in a similar fashion, comparing it to a conveyor belt: monotonous, repetitive, without substance. He goes on to attribute his substandard education to an institutional belief in students' lack of capacity: "students were told that they were failures and would not succeed in life because they were disabled" (*Seed v Ontario*, 2012, para. 25). Some were singled out, for being poor ("This house parent told the poorer students ... that she could do as she pleased because their parents could not afford a lawyer"); or for struggling in school lessons ("his teachers made snide remarks and implied that he had cheated [and students] were made to feel like they were destined for failure") (*Seed v Ontario*, 2012, paras. 34, 68).

Residents' disability marked them for failure, and in turn, marked them as deserving of the treatment they received, such as when staff members told Templin he was worthless, and would never amount to anything (*Templin v Her Majesty the Queen* Statement of Claim, 2016, para. 25). Examples of abusive treatment include staff taking advantage of residents' impairments, by sneaking up on deaf students from behind or throwing heavy objects at blind students (*Welsh v Ontario* Statement of Claim, 2016, para. 3; *Seed v Ontario*, 2012, para. 19). The derogatory perception of disability was pervasively rooted in staff conduct and motivations. *Barker v Barker* offers an overt example of this. The aforementioned Ombudsman Report identifies justification for Oak Ridge experimental treatments: "It can be prescribed for undermining (undesirable destructive words or actions). Should a man not mix or talk or generally interact for more than what is thought to be a desirable period of time, he will go to MAPP" (*Barker v Barker*, 2017, para. 47).[12]

To use Banduran language, distrust and dehumanization operate as cognitive shifts to excuse the abdication of moral precepts. The cognitive mechanism at work changes the perception of the victim, allowing perpetrators to shift blame for violence from themselves onto the victim, or circumstances seemingly created by the dehumanized victim: "violent conduct becomes a justifiable defensive reaction to belligerent provocations. Victims get blamed for bringing suffering on themselves" (Bandura, 2002, p. 110). When incarcerated populations are reimagined – given their dependencies, or their disabilities – as not human, not persons, but simply as sub-human bodies, self-regulation in the treatment of their bodies and the management of their care need not hold, need not guide or keep in check staff conduct. Further, acting out against these forms of control, or enacting embodied forms of resistance, invites additional violence, which reinforces perceptions of savagery and need for bodily containment and constraint.

Conclusions

The potential to enact cruelty is universal and situational. This is a truth we sought to unpack by unearthing in the Institutional Cases particular situations that lose everyday moral inhibitions. We have endeavoured to lay out several institutional conditions that enable moral abdication: reforming residents, limited institutional resources, social and geographical isolation, social hatred and suspicion of residents, and the twinned denial of bodily autonomy through regimented daily routines and unfettered access of staff to incarcerated bodies.

If these conditions are met, the institution is primed to be a site of moral abdication and, accordingly, a place where the potential for deep violence to occur is high. Moral abdication occurs when the overriding goal of the institution is not moral accountability, but rather the instrumental containment and control of an institutional body/object – the rendering of unruly human subjects into inert objects – and this goal is expressed through the conditions so outlined.

Notes

1 Civil litigation is an area of law where aggrieved parties pursue legal action against their aggravators. We are particularly focusing on tort law, or the law of finding and compensating wrongdoing, brought by a class of persons who have shared a common experience of wrongdoing. A note on language: we use terminology like "resident" and "patient" found in case law, but we acknowledge people who were formally institutionalized tend to refer to themselves as "survivors."

2 Zimbardo is relevant to our analysis not only for his insight on situational violence, but also because the Stanford Prison Experiments are a particularly illustrative example of research on human subjects stretching ethical limits. Psychologists of his epoch, like John Zubek and Donald Hebb, were architects of experiments that placed physical and psychological strain on university students in ways that would meet current definitions of torture. Their work paved the way for experimentation on human subjects in institutional settings, conducted by the likes of Cameron Ewen, and medical authorities cited in the Institutional Cases (particularly those featuring Oak Ridge). Thus, in this chapter, we offer a conceptual framework that comes with a rather dark human history, one where the observers of situational violence are themselves implicated in cultivating those conditions. For more, see Gold, 2016.

3 While there are certainly objective morality schemes (e.g., moral philosophies that rest on divine dictates or human rationality), there nevertheless tends to be a social aspect to morality, where a collective of persons agrees to a set of values to guide behaviour. Christian moral codes, for instance, are assumed to have an objective foundation, a foundation that transcends social context, but the codes are nevertheless interpreted through and by church communities.

4 Marilyn and Jim Dolmage acted as litigation guardians, a common occurrence in cases pursued by persons who might lack capacity to understand court proceedings. Christine Clarke, Rosalind Bechard, and Sharon Clegg acted as litigation guardians for David McKillop, Mary Ellen Fox, and Marlene McIntyre, respectively.

38 *Institutional Cases and moral abdication*

5 The facilities entailed are as follows: St. Lawrence Regional Centre, L. S. Penrose Centre, D'Arcy Place, Oxford Regional Centre and Mental Retardation Unit, Midwestern Regional Centre, Adult Occupational Centre, Durham Centre for Developmentally Handicapped, Muskoka Centre, Prince Edward Heights, Northwestern Regional Centre, Bluewater Centre, and Pine Ridge. See *McIntyre v. Ontario*, 2016.

6 A note on name changes across Barker's procedural history: the lead plaintiff, previously cited in the case law as Vance Eggleston, identifies as a trans woman, and changed her name to Shauna Taylor. The challenges Taylor encountered as a trans woman seeking medical accommodations in support of her gender identity and expression in the forensic psychiatric system fall outside the scope of this chapter, but we nevertheless wish to flag their relevance to the central tenets of this book.

7 Templin involves a psychiatric facility, but given the case is so recent, the legal materials generated around this case are limited.

8 This list is not exhaustive. Previous suits lay the groundwork for Institutional Cases, such as *Rumley v. British Columbia*, 2001, involving state negligence around the Jericho Hill School for deaf children. Outside Ontario, albeit not yet available in English translation, a settlement was reached in a class action against a Roman Catholic institution for deaf students (*Centre de la communauté sourde du Montréal métropolitain c. Clercs de Saint-Viateur du Canada*, 2016). Further, we are focusing our analysis on disability, though institutionalization certainly affected other minoritized groups, evidenced in *Elwin v. Nova Scotia Home for Colored Children*, 2013; and *Cloud et al. v. Canada (Attorney General)*, 2004, involving residential schooling of Indigenous children.

9 The three main programs assessed in *Barker* were Defence Disruptive Therapy or DDT, wherein patients were administered hallucinogenic cocktails; the Motivation, Attitude, Participation Program or MAPP, which involved re-educating patients by having them sit in a confined space without moving or speaking for 14 consecutive days; and the Total Encounter Capsule Program, which entailed patients being kept in solitary confinement.

10 "In 1978, the Ombudsman of Ontario commissioned Drs. Butler, Rowsell, and Long to investigate the Social Therapy Unit at Oak Ridge and to evaluate the treatment programs" (*Barker v Barker*, 2017).

11 To launch civil suits, plaintiffs (or those who allege wrongdoing) file a statement of claim. Defendants in turn file a statement of defence to respond to claims point for point. These documents are used to negotiate a settlement through mediation or arbitration, and if this fails they are referred to in court when justices are making determinations.

12 For more on MAPP, see note 9.

3 The institutional violence continuum

In Chapter 2, we examined the organizational traits that lead to moral abdication, and thus violence, within institutional settings. In this chapter, we look closely at practices of institutional violence themselves, and address these questions from a different angle through two linked assertions: first, that within institutions, *care itself* is necessarily a central and operational category of violence; and second, that care *qua* violence is the cultural bedrock upon which more extreme forms of violence rest. In other words, institutional care is, by its very design, a kind of violence, and the omnipresence of care-*qua*-violence is rooted in the dehumanization of institutionalized residents, and marks institutions as spaces where violence is normalized. This provides cultural space and permission for seemingly more egregious types of violence to occur.

To build this argument, we draw from a series of in-depth interviews and ethnographic data collected through the *Recounting Huronia* project described in Chapter One. Using both interview data and ethnographic observation, and drawing from sociologist Michel Wieviorka's (2010) important theoretical contributions regarding situational violence, we propose a continuum for understanding institutional violence, beginning with instrumental, institutionally sanctioned forms of daily care-*qua*-violence and ending with sadistic forms of violence that seem to exist only for the gratification of violence itself. These are not discrete categories, but rather inextricably linked and woven into the very fabric of institutional life. This chapter thus seeks to taxonomize institutional violence in order to understand how and why violence lies at the heart of institutionalization, and thus why the act of incarceration is in and of itself an inevitable act of violence.

This analysis draws from multiple sources of data including ethnographic data from the site visit, narratives gathered in workshop, object analysis utilizing artifacts from Huronia, and in-depth interview data. Before examining these narratives, we want to pause and reflect about the difficulty of including stories of deep violence and trauma within this kind of work. This analysis comes from many years of work with Huronia survivors, including a series of in-depth interviews on their lives while incarcerated. The stories survivors shared were of experiences of incomprehensible violence and cruelty.

40 *The institutional violence continuum*

This work is overtly driven by a desire for justice on behalf of those whose lives have been deeply impacted by experiences of incarceration. Thus, our primary ethical duty is to our survivor colleagues, who feel strongly that their stories should be shared widely with the world. This sharing is a way of resisting the violence that has totalized their life world for so long. We are cognizant, though, that the stories themselves are deeply disturbing at best, traumatizing at worst. In this chapter, we have worked to balance the desires of survivors to share their experiences of violence with the need to respect readers' boundaries regarding the amount and profundity of trauma relayed within this work. However, this analysis includes highly graphic content regarding physical and sexual violence.

Dehumanization

In order to make sense of the role of violence within institutional settings, we approach this analysis from two theoretical perspectives. First, drawing from the work of Goffman (2007), Zimbardo (2007), and Malacrida (2015), we argue that institutional violence is situational, and deeply tied to practices of dehumanization central to the institutional project. Second, drawing from the work of Wieviorka (2009), we assert that violence within institutions may be usefully categorized along a continuum that ranges from instrumental "cold" violence to sadistic "hot" violence.

The centrality of dehumanization as the bedrock of institutional practice is not novel to this work. In his ground breaking early work on asylums, Goffman (1961) writes extensively on the movement of institutional inmates from autonomous or non-institutionalized to an institutionalized member of a group whose autonomy has been stripped. This transition, Goffman writes, is wholly necessary for the functioning of the institution as such: "The handling of many human needs by the bureaucratic organization of whole blocks of people – whether or not this is a necessary or effective means of social organization in the circumstances – is the key fact of total institutions" (p. 6). The creation of "blocks of people" is specifically tied to the institution's perceived need to conduct surveillance over this population as a means of control. He thus demonstrates in this work that total institutions are structurally bound to processes of residents' dehumanization, defined as the unrelenting processes of denigration or "mortification" (p. 22) of residents' bodily and personal integrity, resulting in loss of autonomy.

Malacrida (2012, 2015), who studies the dehumanization of people with intellectual disabilities at the Michener Institute in Alberta, Canada, expands on Goffman's analyses, describing dehumanization as the "process of attributing less-than-human or non-human attributes to the members of a group" (2012, p. 2). Building on Goffman's work, Malacrida analyzes dehumanization within institutions as arising from two key institutional practices: (1) the loss of individuality necessary for institutional care; and (2) the use of surveillance as an operational strategy within the institution.

The routinized processes of dehumanization conducted in institutional spaces – through surveillance, segregation, and control of eating, sleep, education, hygiene, play, and the list goes on and on – impact a person's abilities to develop relationships and skill sets, to accept and execute responsibilities, "in short, how to live as human beings in the world" (2015, p. 91).

As we have noted in Chapter 2, in his work on situational evil – i.e., the kinds of inter-human cruelty that arise from constraining contextual factors rather than individual dispositions – Zimbardo (2007) also recognizes that dehumanization is linked to forms of professional practice, in particular situations that rely on surveillance as a mode of caregiving. He writes: "Sometimes dehumanization serves an adaptive function ... when a job requires processing large number of people in one's caseload or daily schedule ... *Dehumanization typically facilitates abusive and destructive action toward those so objectified*" (p. 223, emphasis added). Therefore, residents' individual selves are superseded by the institutional project of population management for the sake of organizational ease, and so residents are transmuted from individual subjects to objects of institutional interest and control. This erasure of resident subjectivity, we might even say their humanity, is inherently connected to the functioning of the institution. However, given that the humanness, or personhood, of so many institutionalized populations is, from the outset, considered dubious (Malacrida, 2012), the further stripping of human dignity within institutional settings lends itself to less social challenge than with populations whose humanity is not deemed as questionable.

Hot vs. cold violence

Malacrida (2015) moves from an analysis of dehumanization to consideration of the cultures of violence deeply embedded in institutional living. She differentiates between ordinary and extraordinary violence. Violence of the ordinary or quotidian variety may be the result of neglect and injuries sustained from other residents or as a consequence of punishment. Extraordinary or explosive violence, she describes as acts of brutality more common around feeding and toilet times that result in more severe injuries. Her work gestures toward the violence spectrum we are presenting in our own theory of violence, and implies a place for dehumanization as the processes that render a human being, by virtue of having their humanity stripped away, unworthy of protection from violent acts. We might move from here to posit that situational violence can and should be categorized along a continuum, which begins with the dehumanization of institutional care and ends with violence that occurs for its own sake, or for the sake of pleasure. In other words, sadistic end-point violence is only culturally permissible within a context where dehumanized forms of care are the norm.

This analysis is informed by Wieviorka (2010), whose work attempts to categorize and make sense of different types of seemingly incomprehensible, large-scale forms of violence, including torture and war crimes.

42   *The institutional violence continuum*

In particular, he describes violence as twofold. On the one hand, he frames instrumental violence, or violence with a very clear end goal, as a "cold" violence. Cold violence is driven by logic and a given end-point; violence here is thus the mechanism to make something happen, not a goal unto itself. Conversely, Wieviorka introduces "hot" violence, or violence for the sake of violence. This kind of violence may or may not start with a clear or rational end goal, but regardless of its original aim, becomes about excess. Wieviorka includes in this category of violence "cruelty" and "sadism," each of which denotes a kind of pleasure or gratification in inflicting pain.

Wieviorka makes two important analytic links around this "hot" violence. First, he describes the libidinal pleasure created by hot forms of violence, calling this libidinal force *jouissance*: a psychoanalytic term denoting a kind of excessive or frenzied pleasure that occurs outside cultural norms or the limits of social restraint. Second, he describes instances of hot violence as *situational* – as taking place in very particular social circumstances. He writes: "Such phenomena [i.e., acts of "hot" violence or violence for its own sake] appear to result from the activation of hitherto forbidden and hidden archaic or primal drives which are set free *when circumstances allow them to emerge*" (2010, p. 129, emphasis added). Cold forms of violence – beginning with the dehumanization inherent in institutional care – cede to hot forms of violence in particular social circumstances by laying normative cultural groundwork. It is possible to trace how cold violence is tied to increasingly hotter forms within institutions, meaning that extreme and sadistic forms of violence are intrinsically embedded within the organizational structure of the institution itself.

In Huronia, violence did not occur as isolated incidents, but rather as a pervasive, all-encompassing cultural orientation. For example, in interviews with survivors, I (Kate) did not ask a single question about violence beyond clarifying what a survivor recounted. Rather, my interview questions revolved around routines of daily living in the institution, which could not be recounted by a single survivor without a detailed description of multiple kinds of violence inflicted by multiple perpetrators. Thus, this analysis works to organize the violence described by survivors along a continuum, arranged from the most instrumental or cold forms to the hottest or most sadistic.

Cold violence: care as an operational category of violence

We begin with a discussion of cold or instrumental violence. Cold institutional violence comprises forms of violence that are born directly out of the system of institutional care itself. They are thus inadvertently violent, to the extent that they are not wilfully performed as acts of violence and do not consciously produce suffering as a goal unto itself. Rather, these are acts of care and management, often related to the body, which cause suffering as an unintended but nonetheless *necessary* result. These are actions that are

The institutional violence continuum   43

overt, are a legitimate part of professional practice, and are institutionally sanctioned; yet they are not seen or intended as acts of violence themselves. Violence here is a by-product of normal institutional routines. These acts are so inherent and so necessary to the functioning of the institution that they are regarded by internal actors as obvious and unimpeachable solutions to the 'problem' of resident care when the answer to that problem is institutionalization. These types of violent encounters, both omnipresent and 'micro' in nature, degrade individual residents through the negation of individuality, constant bodily surveillance, and, ultimately, the usurpation of agency and dignity.

These acts of care are necessarily tied to processes of dehumanization. For institutions to operate, especially institutions with large population sizes and few staff, daily life must be undertaken as a group endeavour, or *en masse*. This means that individual wants, needs, and desires must be ignored or subsumed in favour of a more efficient group model of care. This model affords no privacy, no choice, and little dignity for residents within its day-to-day interactions. Central to the inherent violence of care within institutions is thus the chronic negation of the individual. Further, care within an institutional context is necessarily not consensual. Care in these settings is neither sought out nor agreed upon by the receiver of care. This means that the caregiving dispensed is inherently violent from the outset.

For example, all activities of daily living at Huronia were structured in a way that served to negate individuality and to remind residents that they were merely part of a herd. Residents ate, slept, and worked as a group. To move from one activity to another, staff demanded that residents line up in military-style single file: to the shower (often naked), from the shower to the dressing area (where they dressed as a group), from the dressing area to the dining room, from the dining room to the school unit, and so on. Residents slept in large wards sometimes housing as many as many as 50 residents to a room; beds were often just inches apart. Residents ate in cafeterias at designated times of day, seated at large dining tables where they were given no choice about what or how much food they were given. Residents recall that their items were labelled with a number rather than a name. Residents did not choose their own clothing, and in fact, did not own personal clothing items per se; rather, residents recall that once a week large piles of laundry were brought to the ward and staff demanded that they rummage for items that might fit. These items of clothing had to be worn for a week before they were taken to be laundered, because the laundry was not done per individual, but in a large, industrial laundry facility. Institutional policy dictated that boys maintain shaved heads (possibly to reduce lice infestations); girls' hairstyles were dictated by the staff (predictably, girls wore their hair longer and styled, despite the equal threat of lice for boys and girls). This model of care seems, from an outside perspective, deeply inhumane, but within the schema of the institution,

44   *The institutional violence continuum*

these are mechanisms which ensure that a large number of people have their basic needs (food, sleep accommodation, hygiene, laundry, etc.) attended to on a regular basis.

A related way in which acts of institutional care double as acts of violence is through the constant surveillance of residents' bodies in order to keep them in a pre-determined state of health and well-being. These acts of surveillance are, as a rule, public, humiliating, and constant. Moreover, acts of surveillance often demand further punitive forms of intervention. For example, both male and female Huronia survivors remember that they were monitored at night by both staff and resident "ward bosses" whose job it was to check that everyone was asleep and to give permission for residents to get up to go to the bathroom. Sometimes, if they were caught awake when they should be sleeping, residents would be punished with physical violence or would not be permitted to use the bathroom. Further, staff forced bed-wetters to sleep in a "wet ward" alongside fellow bed-wetters, where the spectacle of soiled laundry became one that was made humiliatingly public.

Likewise, female survivors remember the shame-inducing ritual of public weighing that happened on a monthly, or sometimes bi-weekly, basis. These public weigh-ins were, ostensibly, to ensure that the girls were neither over- nor underweight, thereby fulfilling the underlying institutional goal of monitoring and maintaining residents' physical health. Thus, these public weigh-ins, and the resultant decisions to increase or reduce food accordingly, were not meant as punishment per se, but rather as an efficient measure of resident care. Of course, to the residents, these weigh-ins felt oppressive. Pam describes her experience:

KATE: And did they ever tell you they were concerned about you getting fat?

PAM: Oh yeah. If you were a little bit more than, if you weighed more than your height what you should weigh, they would starve you to death. You got no bread, you got no potatoes.

KATE: HUH. AND WHEN DID YOU GET WEIGHED?

PAM: The first Sunday of the month. [This was] very scary for me, if I lost weight, I got into trouble.

KATE: What kind of trouble?

PAM: I got punished and I was made to eat double the amount of food.

KATE: And when you were weighed, where were you weighed?

PAM: In the playroom, no, in the hallway at K cottage. The staff [weighed us]. We all had to line up. And they had their charts out and wrote down what we weighed.

KATE: And what's your memory of that?

PAM: Very fearful...'Cause I was afraid I was gonna lose more weight. And I did. No matter how much they gave me to eat, I just kept losing weight.

The institutional violence continuum   45

KATE: And if you were losing weight you were forced to eat more, right?
PAM: Yes. Food that I didn't like. I didn't mind eating more cereal in the morning. I just didn't like eating the lunches and the supper.

Connie also details the humiliating impact of being deemed overweight:

KATE: What if you were at the fat table?
CONNIE: Well you'd get porridge, no milk, an orange, and one piece of toast.
KATE: And how did they know when people were too fat?
CONNIE: They kept a record if you were too—they'd get you on the scale, they'd put you on the scale before you went down to the dining room and they'd weigh you and if you were 120 pounds you were too fat.
KATE: And did that happen every day? Like how often were you weighed?
CONNIE: Every two weeks.
KATE: And who did the weighing?
CONNIE: Miss G [nursing staff].
KATE: And what would happen if she thought that you were too fat?
CONNIE: Well to me, she called me fatty and put me on the fat table.

Similarly, former male survivors detailed shameful instances of bodily surveillance in the name of health preservation in regard to washing. Like most things at Huronia, washing was performed *en masse* in large, open shower rooms, meaning that residents were surveilled both by other residents (washing at the same time) and by staff who monitored bathing activities. In some instances, boys were asked to wash one another in order to ensure that a thorough job had been done. More egregious still were staff concerns regarding the cleanliness of boys' bodies, evidenced by routine post-shower genitalia checks as described by Brian Logie[1]:

KATE: So, regularly you would line up naked for your showers, and after showering somebody would check that you'd done it properly?
BRIAN: Exactly. They would make me, uh uhh I don't want to embarrass you... forgive me for what I'm about to say... They made me pull my foreskin back. They used to grab me and and see, make you know touch it and make sure I did it right. [They] used to make me bend over and uhm show my butt off. And uh, uh most of the times uh they used to make us lean up against the wall. And I didn't like that too much.
KATE: And they, why did you have to lean, lean against the wall?
BRIAN: I have no idea. But we stayed there until afterwards and then this is when I first begin there.
KATE: Yes, so you were very little.

This account is reiterated by Huronia survivor David Houston. Interestingly, in his comment noting that some of the boys were "pretty young" in the

46 *The institutional violence continuum*

institution, David seems to be echoing the institutional ethos that perhaps penis checks were an important method of maintaining standards of hygiene:

KATE: Did they inspect people after their showers?

DAVID: Uhm they always inspected the penis. Especially uncircumcised boys. Pretty much only them. They would say "okay skin 'er back." To see if you washed it. You know, I guess young boys, don't forget some of them are pretty young there.

Tied up both in the negation of individuality and in the constant public surveillance of resident bodies within institutions, and underlying the assertion that care within institutions is inherently violent, are the ways basic measures of humanity – agency, dignity – are apprehended through the design of the institution itself. Of course, this makes sense as a model of efficient care provision. Simply: it is very difficult to run an institutional organization that houses many residents and also maintain the primacy of agency and dignity. It is more laborious to account for different tastes, schedules, sleep patterns, clothing preferences, and need for privacy; and more expensive and difficult to staff an institution where each resident has their own bedroom, access to personal belongings (and space to store them), private bathing quarters, freedom to choose which activities to attend and when to attend them, and enough attendant care to support a dignified and autonomous existence. The argument here is that when human dignity cedes to efficient institutional models of care, care cannot help but be violent in nature.

Warm violence: punishment and the enforcement of care routines

At the limit of cold, or instrumental, violence is "warm" violence. This is violence which is instrumental (or goal-oriented) and to some extent institutionally sanctioned, but an intentional action rather than the unintended by-product of care. Acts of warm violence are self-consciously harmful, undertaken with a particular goal in mind – often behavioural modification. This is to say that warm violence is not violence for its own sake, or for the sake of gratification, but violence meant to enact change or enforce conformity or obedience. Suffering, then, is a necessary and desired outcome of warm violence. Warm violence is linked to the violence of caregiving (i.e., cold violence) as it marks the limit or end-point of caregiving; when caregiving routines fail, or when conformity or obedience to these routines are disrupted and transgressed, cold violence heats up. In other words, warm violence maintains the functionality of cold violence. The word used most often by Huronia survivors to describe warm violence is "punishment," which they detailed in the following ways.

Perhaps most obviously, punishment at Huronia was used to induce behavioural compliance, even when this contravened the needs and desires

The institutional violence continuum 47

of those who were institutionalized. Brian Logie and Stanley describe, in separate examples, how punishment was designed to produce behavioural compliance:

BRIAN: No, this was uh, this was several times with that damn cribbage board. I hate cribbage boards to this very day. They never beat us on the arms or legs or stuff, it was always on the bottom of the feet, I couldn't figure it out. Well the only time they were any good to us was, after awhile I just, I just, I just well actually I just complied with what they wanted.

STANLEY: And I was the only one who did not want to say grace, so I didn't stand up and you know they didn't, the staff didn't like that, so they would ask me to stand up and and say it and then they would take the melamine cup and throw it at ya. One of those melamine cups and then they would come and take your plate and put it on the floor and make you lie on your stomach with your hands behind your back, it was called digging worms. Digging worms, yep. And that's not the kind of worms for fishing by the way. And they would put the plate underneath your mouth and they'd take their foot and push your face in it. It only happened to me once.

Punishment was the first response to defiance, resistance, or acting out. Acting out took many forms in Huronia, from mundane instances of "mouthing off" or disrespecting staff to more serious occurrences like attempting to run away. Some residents even reported attempts to fight, harm, or even kill staff who had been particularly abusive. Regardless, real or perceived impudence was met with severe retribution. Often, responses to acting out were both vicious and public, so as to set an example for other residents. One particularly common punishment was to force residents to clean the institution with a toothbrush or with a very heavy push broom called a rubber. Residents often had to perform these intense forms of cleaning for extended periods of time – days, or even weeks, often night and day. Sometimes they were forced to perform these duties clothed only in a nightgown:

DAVID: You had to hold your arms out and with a broom on it for, try holding that there for an hour and it just feels like it's 100 pounds, weighs 100 pounds and... Like with your hands straight out and someone would put a straw corn broom and you're holding it with your arms. Now as soon as that goes on your arms there the first five minutes is fine but 1/2 hour goes by it feels like you got 100 pounds there on ya. If you lower your hands you'd get a smack in the back of the head or... and why did you have to do that? You did something, stupid or maybe out of line or something.

Isolation was used as a punishment to contain particularly unruly residents. Isolation took several forms. The judicious use of "side rooms" and "pipe rooms" – windowless rooms or utility closets – functioned as a method of inflicting solitary confinement. Many residents speak of spending prolonged

48 *The institutional violence continuum*

periods in side rooms where there was simply a mattress on the floor and nothing to do during confinement. Likewise, residents were confined using strait jackets:

CONNIE: Well, I had a best friend there and she was, I knew her when I was at [Huronia] and she got up and grabbed a knife off the table and stabbed Mrs. X. And then she said, "Jenny told me to do it." She took the knife to Mrs. X, Mrs. X threw her to the floor, put her foot to her face and smashed her face to the floor, you couldn't see no white in her face. My punishment was to change her you-know-what and take her to the toilet bath and change her you-know-what. I didn't mind doing it because she was my best friend...her whole face was blue, her whole face... It wasn't even a sharp knife it was a butter knife and then they put a strait jacket on her. That's why I had to clean because she couldn't do it with a strait jacket.

Figure 3.1 An image from the Huronia Regional Centre of a "side room" – a space in the institution used for the solitary confinement of residents, sometimes for days at a time.
Photographer Marilyn Dolmage.

The institutional violence continuum 49

Brutality was also deployed to establish social hierarchies among residents. Sometimes social hierarchies were made through staff favouritism: many staff had "pets" they liked more and treated better. Just as often, though, the institution's hierarchicalization was cultivated through staff demanding that residents enact violence as punishment upon one another. Occasionally, these two efforts at dividing the resident population collided, when staff pets were singled out to carry out extreme forms of violence against less favoured residents on behalf of staff. One survivor recalls that staff "pets" were told to push her down the stairs – a fall that resulted in bone fractures that have given her lifelong chronic pain. Pam understands her own turn toward violence as linked to staff-induced forms of aggression:

PAM: I learned to hit back. The staff instigated fights between us in the education unit. When we lined up for punishment facing each other we hit people on the back who were being punished – it was called the tunnel. We would line up 15 people against each other, facing one another, and the people that were on punishment had to crawl through on their hands and knees and get slapped on the back. Yeah, we were trained to hit one another... You did what you were told.

Particularly vicious staff also used punishment, or the threat of it, to create and maintain silence. For example, the resident population – especially younger residents who had more frequent family visits – would not talk openly about their poor living conditions or more egregious forms of violence they had witnessed. Residents were subjected not only to physical brutality (such as beatings) by staff but also chemical constraint (the use of inappropriate overmedication with extremely strong psychotropic and anti-convulsant drugs, generally administered by nurses or other staff) to induce catatonic states. Naturally, these substances had many side effects beyond catatonia; generally, complaints included stomach upset and very sensitive skin. Medication side effects were sadistically utilized by staff as a means of further inducing physical discomfort; medicated residents, for example, remember being forced to sit outside until they sustained severe medication-induced sunburns or were physically ill:

CONNIE: I got Paraldehyde. It's another narcotic to keep your mouth shut and knock you out kind of thing. It's a narcotic given to people; it smells like bubble gum but it burns your stomach and you have to swallow it and if you throw up you get more.

Because the institutions oversaw the corporeal care of residents, bodily functions were a site of intense scrutiny and interest. Ironically, the design

50　*The institutional violence continuum*

of the institution itself contributed to the messiness of institutionalized bodies. Simply, bodies that are routinely brutalized, over-medicated, badly fed, and given no privacy cannot help but erupt and explode – a bodily response met with extreme institutional rejoinders. Connie recalls the following incident:

CONNIE: Because ... well what happened with that one is that I dirtied my pants by mistake – something they gave me to eat didn't agree with me and then they rubbed it in my face and put me in a cold tub. Two on this side, two on that side and Mrs. G. held my head down and put the water with the ice cubes ... I was freezing ... then they put me ... I had to sit for half an hour in there and when I got out they put a ticking dress on me.

While degradation played a role in most forms of punishment and operated as the by-product to loss of bodily control, there were instances where robbing residents of dignity seemed to be the central goal of the punishment, bearing little to no correspondence to the triggering event. Humiliation was a method of control but also an occupational ethos in the institution. Consider the following example:

KATE: What did you guys do in the playroom?
MARGARET: Well there was a staff in there all of the time with us. We would play and uh there was a couple of staff, one staff if we uh, got talking she'd make us get up and pull our pants down and walk around the playroom with our pants down.

Finally, punishment was used as a way to remind residents about the limits of their humanity. This is to say that death, and the threat of death, was omnipresent within the institutional setting. This was not simply because residents died while incarcerated; death was used as a kind of threat, as if the institution enjoyed instilling in residents a sense of the limits of their humanity, the outer reaches of punishment. The threat of death reminded residents that the institution was all-powerful and could end life just as well as it could sustain life. Residents recall being taken to watch animals being slaughtered on Huronia's farm following perceived misbehaviour. Similarly, some residents were taken to the in-house morgue and forced to clean bodies, or to clean around bodies awaiting burial. Sometimes staff used the fear of death rather than death itself, telling residents that the labyrinthine tunnel system below the institution was full of garbage bags of bodies. This did not feel like an idle threat given so many residents died at Huronia, that the institution housed its own graveyard where residents were unceremoniously buried.

Figure 3.2 An underground tunnel in the Huronia Regional Centre that linked multiple buildings across the campus. Survivors describe sadistic violence occurring in the tunnel system.
Photographer Jen Rinaldi.

Hot violence: the inevitability of sadism

Hot violence is violence that exists for its own sake, or for the sake of pleasure. These are forms of violence that exist purely for themselves and for the pleasure of doing violence to others, otherwise termed sadism. Here, suffering and the gratification of violence are not attached to an instrumental goal and are not a by-product (intentional or not), but rather are the *only goal*. These forms of violence are not part of professional practice and not officially sanctioned activities; but regardless of their non-official capacity, they are very much part of the institutional fabric. These acts may be public insofar as they are part of the acknowledged cultural milieu, but may also be private, or have an air of secrecy about them. These acts may be perpetrated by residents and staff alike.

These sorts of violent encounters upon public revelation are the most profoundly shocking and unimaginable because they are not attached to an underlying logic of behaviour modification or discipline; however, it is crucial to recognize that they are inextricably linked to the other two forms of violence – without which hot or sadistic violence would have no fertile cultural ground from which to grow. This is to say that, if the institutional model inherently creates violence through care and punishment, then the cultural fabric of the

52 *The institutional violence continuum*

institution is one in which violence is not just normalized and sanctioned, but indeed, absolutely essential to its existence. It is in such spaces that hot violence flourishes not as the aberrant actions of a few unhinged individuals but as a *cultural practice*. In this sense, instances of hot violence should come as no surprise at all; indeed, this kind of violence, while horrific, is both routine and predictable within institutional settings like Huronia.

While physical brutality (beatings, whippings, enforced physical labour, and solitary confinement) occurred regularly as part of larger, sanctioned punishment regimens, physical altercations also occurred for no reason at all beyond staff and residents' pleasure of enacting, witnessing, or inciting violence. Stanley, for example, recalls staff-induced fights between residents that served no purpose beyond staff enjoyment:

STANLEY: Ya, I meant uh you know the staff would want to... they would wanna use us for entertainment. Well they always wanted us to fight. And they would always encourage us to fight. And we were always told that if we didn't wanna fight we had to fight with a staff member and we may end up with a broken arm or broken leg or whatever. We would always be hurt.

KATE: And, hang on, do you mean fight with one another?

STANLEY: Ya. I and they had, they already had this one boy that wanted to fight, and I did not want to fight at all. And, so, I found a way and I did it on my own, I found a way to kill the fight in a split second.

KATE: And so how, how did they ask you to fight, how did that happen?

STANLEY: Well they just, they just encouraged us, and they stood around and if you didn't wanna do it they'd push ya into doing it.

An account of hot institutional violence would be incomplete without the inclusion of sexual abuse and sadism, which was an absolutely inescapable facet of life at Huronia. So routine was sexual abuse, that one survivor questioned why I (KR) had not asked about sexual abuse directly in my interview about daily living practices. It was clear to him that you could not talk about daily life at Huronia without talking about sexual abuse, brutal and enduring, perpetrated by staff and by other residents alike. Some residents, particularly those who were able-bodied and who had little contact with the outside world, experienced abuse so severe that it can only be described as sexual torture. For these residents, sexual abuse at the hands of staff has left indelible physical and emotional scars that shape every aspect of their current daily lives: phobias, flashbacks, nightmares, dissociation, and physical pain from particularly violent sexual episodes all mar their post-institutional experience. Residents who did not endure the same depth and profundity of violation struggle with the terror of witnessing, even obliquely, this kind of suffering, and guilt for having escaped this treatment while others around them were brutalized. Some residents struggle with themselves having perpetrated further violence, both physical and sexual, while at the institution.

Sometimes sadistic, or hot, forms of violence were tied to punishment, but traversed the line between punishment and pleasure. For example, both

The institutional violence continuum 53

former staff and residents remember instances where particularly unruly female residents were "handed over" to male staff members for punishment. The punishment was rape:

CONNIE: Well, my girlfriend [Donna], I and Miss G [female nursing staff] and Mr. M [male staff] were friends. Me and Donna were called down to Mr. M's office. I went in first and he shut the door and said, "you know why you're here," and I said, "no," and he said "I'm a social worker." I said, "oh, what did I do?" He says what you're gonna do. I go, "what am I gonna do?" And he pulled down his zipper and he puts you know what in my mouth and he told me what to do and I did it and I had to swallow you know what and then he threw me down on the chair and then he put it in my you know what. They hurt me. He didn't put it right in, kind of thing, enough that it would hurt, like I felt pain. And then he (indistinct) go, "You open your mouth you will be punished." Miss G won't let me out. So, I went out crying and Donna said, "What happened?" and I said, "I can't tell you," and she went in and he did the same to her. She came out crying and I says, "now you know what happened."

Similarly, Brian Logie's recollection of hot violence was inextricably linked to both cold and warm forms of violence. In this quote, Brian makes clear that his sexual abuse was tied to caregiving routines (nighttime surveillance), punishment (to enforce behavioural compliance), and the perpetrator's sexual gratification:

KATE: Okay. So, you slept naked?
BRIAN: Yes ma'am.
KATE: Mmhrmm...
BRIAN: And the housecoat, I remember wearing this housecoat a lot and we used to go to the bathroom, we used to ask permission to go to the bathroom and the caretaker would come and help us. That, I didn't like at all. 'Cause he sat me on the toilet after I went to the bathroom, he'd just sit me on there and ask me to do things to him. And, uh, so I did what he asked me to do because I didn't want to be beat no more. He brought me different things, he brought me chocolate bars, he brought me stuff, used to sit me on his knee saying, "you're my boy."

Other forms of sexual violence were not even obliquely tied to the functioning of the institution, but rather simply occurred as a matter of course. Brian and Connie both recall their experiences of sexual abuse as ongoing, even routinized, and unattached to any other reason other than the gratification of sexual violence. Brian reflects:

But they still have no excuse for what they did to me up there. I mean, to rape somebody on a weekly basis, that's not fair.

54 *The institutional violence continuum*

This kind of sexual violence, of course, is the paragon of violence that has no connection to the creation of efficiency, order, or discipline, but simply is cruelty for the sake of pleasure. It is the end result of an institutional setting in which residents' subjectivity has been obliterated and they have been re-imagined as institutional objects to which anything can be done. This is what happens when institutions are the site of dehumanized forms of care.

Symbolic violence

A final category of violence exists in the institution that must be added to complete this analysis: symbolic violence, and in particular, the violence committed against the bodies of institutional residents who perished while in care. This is a particularly important type of violence because, while the treatment of non-living bodies in the institution did not cause physical pain or suffering per se, these actions form a powerful symbolic message regarding the humanity of residents. Human beings take care of other human remains as a marker of respect and a way of creating and maintaining shared community and social solidarity. Across cultures, human remains are treated with dignity – they are consecrated, they are sacred. The desecration of human remains is an act of deepest disrespect saved for enemies and others considered less-than-human. In other words, to desecrate the dead is to do a kind of deep violence against their very human-ness. Regarding Lacan's analysis of the symbolic importance of burial rights Philippe Van Haute (1998) writes: "the burial place… is the first symbol in which humanity can recognize itself. Only humans bury their dead and erect monuments to them because only humans are in the full sense of the word 'mortal'" (p. 113). And yet, Huronia residents remain forgotten, unnamed and therefore unpreserved as human subjects, denied their humanity.

Residents who died at Huronia – and indeed, there were thousands – were treated to undignified ends in multiple ways. Dead resident bodies were used as a form of punishment for living residents: survivors recall staff forcing them to look dead bodies, or to clean around dead bodies in the morgue as a punitive measure meant to frighten. But perhaps more shocking is the ongoing management of survivor remains. Residents who died at Huronia were buried only in graves marked with small, numbered gravestones, and were thus not afforded the dignity of named burial sites. Further, throughout the latter part of Huronia's history, these gravestones were dug up and repurposed as paving stones for a walkway, leaving the dead with no monument at all. On a practical level, this of course makes it extremely difficult for family members to visit and pay respect to deceased residents – so residents remain isolated and alone even in death.

The cemetery at Huronia remains a site of activity and community engagement. Survivors visit the cemetery regularly and try to upkeep what is left of this site as an act of respect for those who did not survive Huronia. They have written songs in honour of the dead, pledging that their deaths will not be in vain, that their suffering will be remembered. There is political and community activism at work by survivors and remaining family members alike to match those buried in the cemetery with a name and history. The cemetery has been a point of solidarity between survivors, and a way to make meaning from the enduring pain of surviving institutionalization. This, of course, does not undo the violence committed, but rather draws attention to the profundity of this violence, and struggles to make visible those whom symbolic violence have worked to erase.

Conclusions

Survivor narratives lay bare the spectrum of violence experienced within institutional walls: the inherent violent quality to care and punishment, and the inevitability that these forms of violence give way to sadism. Our taxonomy is fashioned not to organize acts of institutional violence into discrete classifications, for the blurring of the lines between, for example, dehumanizing control over corporeal function and humiliating punishment for lack of bodily control, or forcing residents to punish one another and forcing residents to fight one another, illustrates that these acts slide along a continuum that can dull a person's abhorrence to cruelty. The line moral agents draw for themselves continues to be redrawn in contexts like institutional settings, where cultures of violence define their closed systems of logic. As the interviews conducted for this project make clear, violence was endemic to Huronia: routinized, normalized, structurally essential to Huronia's operations; and as we have sought to demonstrate, such a culture of violence is not an outlier, but is instead common to institutions beyond Huronia.

How, then, do we rewrite this script? We might begin with care, which is possible to enact in non-violent ways, not tied to the violent structure of the institution and not reliant on processes of dehumanization. Examples include community treatment models like the faith-based organization L'Arche that supports persons with intellectual disabilities, or Hogeway Amsterdam's "Dementia Village," or Camphill Communities Ontario's project of facilitating residential lifestyles for persons with intellectual disabilities. All have in common the refusal to erase individuality in the service of efficiency, and a commitment to community engagement instead of isolation. By curtailing instances of cold violence as an operational mechanism, there is far less opportunity in these spaces for violence to heat up, or for violence to spring up for punitive or sadistic reasons.

Note

1 It is important to note that while some survivors who took part in this project wanted to remain anonymous, some felt very strongly that their whole name be associated with the project and with their quotes. Both Brian Logie and David Houston requested that they *not* be anonymous.

4 Thoughtlessness and violence as work culture

This chapter shores up accounts given by staff and administrators of Schedule 1 facilities in Ontario, as well as their relatives, who justify their violent conduct as care; and draws from political philosophy, particularly Hannah Arendt, to treat these accounts to critical analysis. The closing of the Huronia Regional Centre, and the string of lawsuits Patricia Seth and Marie Slark catalysed, opened up discourses on the legacy of institutionalization and how the goings-on within institutions would be remembered, documented, and archived. While Huronia's history has been lately told by survivors, former staff have objected that survivor accounts have been reductionist, or have focused only on the worst, most spectacular examples of institutional conditions and treatment. *Wait*, so the gist of the objection goes: *it wasn't all so bad*.

In legal defences and opinion editorials from the perspectives of staff, we find our attention drawn to the good, or justification for institutional conditions and protocol. Staff defences distance moral actors from violent acts of the institution, and conceptualize institutional violence as exceptional. The incommensurability of staff perspective with institutional survivors' testimony calls for a closer reading of how staff is defining violence, and bracketing out their role in its perpetuation. Exploring narrow conceptualizations of institutional violence as imagined by staff sheds light on how staff operated, and still operate, as moral actors in relationship to violence.

In this chapter, we deconstruct narrow and spectacularized imaginaries of institutional violence using Hannah Arendt's work, particularly her interest in how totalitarian mentalities fold moral actors into administrative machinery that diffuses responsibility for the violence inflicted. To be a cog in the machinery requires a commitment to thoughtlessness, or a lack of criticality – a phenomenon that has been popularly referred to as the *banality of evil*. We follow through on Arendt's call to resist all impulses to mythologize the horrible in our analysis of institutional violence as a thought-defying milieu.

We begin with conceptual scaffolding that takes Arendt as its foundation. We here demonstrate her applications to theories of institutional behaviour. We next consider how staff and their family members characterize their

Thoughtlessness and violence as work culture 57

emplacement in institutional history, and how underscoring their accounts is a particular understanding of violence that does not track with the forms of violence theorized in this book so far. Namely, that violence from the instrumental and ordinary to the sadistic and extreme was a chronic feature of institutional life, that violence was coded as discipline and care, and that institutionalization itself constitutes violence. Using Arendt, we consider how it is possible to arrive at the mindset that one is absolved of the violence inherent to the machinery of the institution. This chapter closes by considering the impossibility of using legal instruments to approach evil, or violence, in its most banal terms, and the problem of demythologizing victim affect.

Theoretical framework

When theorizing violence and its role in the political sphere, Hannah Arendt (1970) is careful to note that power and violence are distinct, despite their tendency to appear together. In this, she departs from thinkers like C. Wright Mills, Max Weber, and Walter Benjamin, who characterize all politics as a struggle for power, and thus all power as a form of violence. She finds "the convention very strange" (p. 35), because reaching such a conclusion requires the premise that the state is entirely an instrument of oppression. To the contrary, for Arendt, governance is not solely or all the way down coercive. Yet, if power does not equate to violence but often appears alongside it, then she is left with the task of distinguishing them, and explaining their relationship.

Violence is a form of exerting or claiming power over another or others. It is an expression of, or a reaction to, power dynamics. To the extent that this is the case, power is not a property of individuals, but the terms of a relationship. Referring to governance, Arendt understands power to correspond "with the human ability not just to act but to act in concert" (p. 45), meaning that power – its distributions, transferences, and investments – is measured and charted by who is in agreement, who is convinced. Violence is thus one way of asserting power, of imposing it, and of claiming it. In the case of those who are in positions of power, violence is a way of inscribing and reinforcing the terms to relationships; and for those who lack power, violence may be a means of disrupting those terms.

Violence requires "the technical development of ... implements" (p. 3). In other words, violence is enacted through tools and techniques. Extending this idea, Elaine Scarry (1985) considers how everyday objects, whatever their original purpose, may be transformed through their practice, their use, as implements of violence. In institutional conditions, such implements are myriad in form: hammers, books, and other such heavy objects; cold water and the thermometers and hoses involved in their production; cloth and cuffs and locked rooms that come to be the tools of restraint; a hand for slapping or foot for stomping.

58 *Thoughtless and violence as work culture*

Controversially, violence for Arendt is also "by nature instrumental" (1970, p. 51). Meaning, violence necessarily involves purpose. Even in moments of seemingly irrational forms of violence – the examples she uses refer to open rebellion in reaction to people or systems in positions of power – the lack of deliberation involved does not negate that there is an end or aim to the outburst. Violence is instrumental to establishing or interrupting the conditions of power. Michel Wieviorka (2010) holds reservations regarding this limited envisioning of violence, and instead places Arendt's cold articulation of violence on a spectrum – as we have analyzed in previous chapters – in contrast with hotter forms of violence that lack intended purposes, even if their effect impacts power relations.

Arendt's fascination with cold violence is nevertheless worth acknowledging for its centrality to her most seminal work, on the trial of former Nazi Adolf Eichmann. Of particular interest to her is Eichmann's trial in Jerusalem, throughout which he refused to take responsibility for his role in the genocide of European Jews, despite being confronted with a parade of witnesses who had survived the Holocaust. Reflecting on his administrative role, which essentially involved the paperwork on deportations to concentration camps, particularly death camps, Eichmann pleaded:

> With the killing of Jews, I had nothing to do. I never killed a Jew, or a non-Jew, for that matter – I never killed any human being. I never gave an order to kill either a Jew or a non-Jew; I just did not do it.
>
> (cited in Arendt, 1963, p. 3)

When recounting how he had to process Hitler's order calling for the physical extermination of the Jews, he himself had "never thought of … such a solution through violence" (p. 31).

Observing the trial, frustrated with and fascinated by Eichmann's refusal of guilt or remorse, Arendt famously coins the term the *banality of evil*. By "banality" she is referring to his lack of machination, or any of the designs that would portray Eichmann as cartoonishly monstrous. The violence for which he was responsible was not rooted in racial hatred; he and the system of government within which he operated normalized and rationalized violence, and rendered it mundane. That his actions and decisions contributed to genocide was lost in his ledger. Neither his history, his family life, his predispositions regarding racial and religious minorities, nor his particular values and politics, bore any indication that he was capable of playing a role in mass violence. It remained entirely unclear to him why he should bear responsibility for his role in state machinery when he understood his actions to be nothing more than following orders and rules.

Arendt explains: "He merely, to put the matter colloquially, never realized what he was doing" (1963, p. 134). She calls this a "lack of imagination" (p. 134), or "sheer thoughtlessness" (p. 134), in that Eichmann acted without thinking about the implications or impacts of his actions. The *banality of evil*

Thoughtlessness and violence as work culture 59

Arendt theorizes is thus itself monstrous, in that it is "word-and-thought-defying" (p. 118). It is an evil that any moral actor is capable of committing, provided they act without thinking. From this perspective, Nazis were not all inherently sadistic, and not destined or doomed to be murderers; their moral centres were not broken from the start. To the contrary, they were brought up in (and brought into) a cultural milieu that prioritized obedience, that compartmentalized their roles and justified their behaviours and actions with enough force and regularity that they found themselves redrawing their lines of acceptable practice. Arendt comments on this moral shift: "so instead of saying: 'What horrible things I did to people!' The murderer would be able to say: 'What horrible things I had to watch in the pursuance of my duties; how heavily the task weighed upon my shoulders'" (p. 106).

Such a moral shift reflects a lack of conscience. Through thinking, moral actors develop conscience, or an internal evaluative check. Conscience is the silent, personal dialogue that takes place within the self, living in acts of thinking. Internal moments of conscience for Arendt may be externalized as judgment, or "the manifestation of the wind of thought" (1978, p. 193). If thought is given the chance to wind, to meander, it might stray away from the world of the self and arrive at the perspectives and positions of others. Thus (at the risk of mixing our metaphors), good judgment involves attempts to "go visiting" (1982, p. 43), a term Arendt uses when referring to empathetic imagining. Eichmann was capable of evil, capable of anything, insofar as he was capable of acting without exercising judgment, or acting without imagining where and on whom his enactments land. His failure to develop the quality of his conscience, and by extension his judgment, was possible because he operated in a space that discouraged thinking and rewarded acts committed absent of thought. Arendt explains: "As Eichmann told it, the most potent factor in the soothing of his own conscience was the simple fact that he could see no one, no one at all, who actually was against the Final Solution" (1963, p. 116).

While Arendt was interested in the role moral agents play in totalitarian regimes like Nazi Germany, or how violence unfolds in wider political arenas, her work has relevance when we sketch out the situational conditions for violence that are common to institutional settings. Chapman (2010), for instance, calls on Arendt to make sense of his role as a residential counsellor at a treatment centre that serviced 'troubled' Indigenous youths. Chapman considers how he pursued this line of employment for political reasons, namely to help the disadvantaged. In his own words: "As I understood it then, I was actually making a difference in the real lives of survivors of family and colonial violence" (p. 5).

In the treatment centre, the use of restraint was common, and not questioned; staff like Chapman regarded the practice as "an unfortunate aspect of the job" (p. 6). It was understood to be unfortunate because staff were aware the practice was traumatic for residents, but still a necessary feature to institutional life. He and colleagues failed to collectively imagine

60 *Thoughtless and violence as work culture*

alternative strategies of care, for "the idea that there could be a world without restraints and locked confinement seemed clearly untrue, as evidenced by the children we worked with" (p. 6). In their rationalization that restraint was an appropriate response to the violent behaviours of residents, they also failed to imagine the roots of those behaviours as a "response to our structural, epistemic, and individual violence" (p. 6). Chapman refers here to a workplace milieu that limited his imaginary capacity. Restraint was enacted absent thought.

Chapman distinguishes his mentality from Adolf Eichmann insofar as Chapman and his fellow treatment centre staff felt they had forged deep and meaningful relationships with residents in their care. While Eichmann and his ilk exercised no judgment over their actions as long as they disregarded the human implications of their paperwork, Chapman and his colleagues regarded those over whom they held power like family. Here, we think Chapman would agree that, despite being a feature that distinguishes the institution from the historic authoritarian regime, the framing of institutional residents as family reinforced thoughtlessness. Even if staff are reluctant to admit they participated in the dehumanization of those in their care, the act of bringing them into the fold as family carried a necessary infantilizing and paternalizing effect. When objectors "asked about what we did in calm, articulate, curious ways, or through tears, even then we were entirely sure about the morality of what we were doing or at least its inevitability" (p. 9).

For Chapman, the attrition of his faculty of thinking was challenged when confronted with people who operated outside the logic of the institution. He recalls a new staff member arriving on her first day of work at the institution and witnessing for the first time the restraining of a resident. The new staff member's reaction marked the event as violent. Protocol dictated that Chapman, as senior staff, approach junior staff to debrief following incidents of restraint – an act designed to "depoliticiz[e] her response as psychological and requiring correction, rather than ethical or political" (p. 10). Protocol like this engendered thoughtlessness, and in so doing clipped the conditions necessary for developing personal conscience and exercising judgment. Instead of submitting to the debrief, however, the new staff member "gathered up her stuff and said, 'That was horrible, I can't do this,' and she left, tears in her eyes" (p. 10). She had not operated in the treatment facility long enough for its conditions to engender thoughtlessness in her, so she still heard the call of conscience. She understood the act she witnessed was violent, "horrible" she called it, because her thoughts drifted to the perspective of the resident – she could imagine the impacts of the act.

Approaching staff and family accounts

Our research project focused on and worked with survivors of institutional violence, rather than engaging former staff of these institutions. This is because our research was rooted in the premise that we believe survivor

Thoughtlessness and violence as work culture 61

accounts, so documenting their experiences in relation to violence did not need to be balanced against the experiences of perpetrators. Further, prioritizing survivors required that we not alienate or re-traumatize them by bringing into our research practices and outputs the perspectives of a survivor's tormentors. It is for these reasons that the data we analyze in this chapter do not derive from first-hand research. Instead, our data here consists in accounts of institutional conditions, especially staff treatment found in the public sphere, usually as objections to survivors' legal and political accomplishments.

For instance, former staff of the Huronia Regional Centre and the general public reacted to the release of Thelma Wheatley's 2013 book, *And Neither Have I Wings to Fly*, which described abusive institutional conditions experienced by Huronia survivors (Bell, 2013). Others reacted to stories relating to the settlement of the class action lawsuit against the government of Ontario (CBC News, 2013). Further, there are instances where former staff moved from commenting on stories to becoming news. In Smith Falls Ontario, former staff of the Rideau Regional Centre (an institution referenced in an early Institutional Case) publicly opposed a settlement arrangement of installing on public property a plaque relating that people had endured abusive conditions while institutionalized at Rideau (Sansome, 2014). Their opposition work crystallized in a circulated petition calling for a public apology to staff whose names had been slandered by general descriptions of institutional abuse (Roy, 2015).

Most staff and family provided their full names, and their stories are a matter of public record, having been published in news articles. Some names given on comment boards related to news articles are anonymous, and there is no guarantee that the full names given on comment boards are accurate since journalists do not verify names on story comment boards. Further, stories related in news article comment boards have not been vetted, but it would be difficult to produce reasons for someone to lie about at least being staff or being family of staff in order to react to allegations of abusive conduct. Their inclusion in a publicly distributed document points to the colour of backlash regardless, and illustrates the arguments that have been entertained in response to recounting institutional violence.

Several narratives in these news clippings begin with a declaration of time spent in the employ of a Schedule 1 facility: 20 years for Marilyn Clements and her husband (Bell, 2013, comment board), 26 for Mary-Anne Gibson (Roy, 2015), 30 for Eileen Whitmore (ibid.), 37 for Donna Porubovic (ibid.). Reference to time has the effect of positioning staff as experts given the weight of their experience. That they experienced, inflicted, and witnessed nothing they would characterize as abuse is meant to relegate narratives of violence to the realm of the anecdotal. Reference to the length of their professional record also has the implied effect of separating out veteran, respected staff from the outliers responsible for anecdotal moments of abuse – the 'bad apples.'

62 *Thoughtless and violence as work culture*

A common theme running through public reactions to residents' allegations of abuse in institutions involves the distancing of self and family from allegations of violent conduct, and even bearing witness to violence. Marilyn Clements positions herself and her husband as former Huronia staff, and declares neither "saw abuse" (cited in Bell, 2013, comment board). Sheila Sansome, whose mother worked at Rideau, articulates, "In my opinion, very little abuse occurred" (2014, para. 1). Deb Stead of Rideau, referring to the difference in conditions prior to and following the release of the 1971 Williston Report and the 1973 Welch Report, speculated: "I think once the government knew better they did better" (cited in Roy, 2015, para. 4). Her interpretation of the history of Schedule 1 facilities contrasted with the use of the Williston and Welch reports as evidence in the class action suit – evidence both of abuse, and that the government of Ontario and the facilities it managed were aware of abusive conditions. The argument in class actions cited Williston and Welch precisely to claim that violence persisted following, and notwithstanding, their reports.

That former staff and their family carry no memory of violence in 20–30-year tenures at institutions seems to signal a perceptual problem when contrasted with survivor testimony that Ontario institutions were places known for their routine abuse. We suggest, animated by Arendt, that staff simply did not regard as violent what they witnessed and enacted, because the conditions within which they operated fostered a culture of thoughtlessness. At the very least, backlash against survivor narratives indicates a failure in empathy, a failure to imagine what institutional living would feel like from the vantage point of the institutionalized.

Public reactions from staff and family reinforce this failure to "go visiting" when they justify staff conduct as a necessary and unfortunate feature of institutional life – necessary and unfortunate because of resident conduct. Says Clements: "I never saw any abuse, unless it was committed by the client" (cited in Bell, 2013, comment board). Here, we see how violence is coded as belonging to the actions of the institutionalized. In contrast to the outbursts of residents, staff did not regard their own protocol and conduct as violent; they instead sanitized their actions as punishment, treatment, and management. The violence of residents is at once narrowing what violence can be, stripping it of its ethical weight, the possibilities of it existing in frustration over indignity or injustice; and justifying the actions of those in power as the means to contain violence rather than acts of violence in themselves.

Overwhelmingly, rather than focusing on the difficult aspects of staff–resident relations, staff accounts tend to frame their relationships positively. Says a staff member who worked at Huronia as a physiotherapist: "I remember some happy residents and some dedicated staff trying to keep them as physically capable as possible" (cited in CBC News, 2013, comment board). Sansome says of her mother: "she went above and beyond the call of duty to make life as pleasant as possible for residents there" (2014, para. 3).

Of those calling for a public apology to staff, Porubovic claims, "over the thousands of staff, probably 75 percent have a story to tell" (cited in Roy, 2015, para. 11). David Johnston goes so far as to "thank the overwhelming majority of staff for their work, commitment, and compassion over the years for the clients in their care" (cited in Roy, 2015, para. 6).

Burghardt (2016) grappled with irreconcilable contrasts in staff and survivor interpretations of institutional conditions. She found staff referencing residents living their best possible lives when she interviewed Huronia staff for an academic study. One interview participant claimed, for instance: "The residents lacked for nothing ... there were so many options for them" (p. 9). She also found overwhelmingly that staff regarded residents as family: "one former staff became visibly distraught over the losses she had suffered due to institutional closure – the loss of relationships with her 'family' of institutional residents, the loss of relationships with colleagues, and the loss of a place of employment" (p. 13). That relationships felt like family seemed to sidestep or absolve their power imbalances, for family structure – especially parent–child relationships when children are young – necessarily carries power imbalances for the sake of ensuring children's care and safety.

And, indeed, the framing device of family was a running theme through former staff accounts. Sansome says of her mother: "she loved them like her own children and she wasn't the only staff member working there who felt the same way" (2014, para. 4). "They came to be family" (cited in Roy, 2015, para. 19), Gibson declared, as did former Rideau staff and present Regional Vice-President of OPSEU Region 4 (a union that represents caretakers): "It was truly a home and that home was made a home by the caring staff" (cited in Roy, 2015, para. 9). Such a framing device blurs the line of caregiving work and, however genuinely or earnestly felt, reinforces paternalistic engagement. It is also especially troubling given that institutionalization isolates disabled persons from their families and communities; claiming institutionalized persons as part of one's family signals co-optation, and eclipses the ways in which the practice of institutionalization separates and disrupts family life.

Law and victim affect

This chapter, and more broadly this book, brings moral and legal theory and social psychology to bear on the conditions of institutional violence. Our theory of violence accounts for the circumstances that bring it about, the role of the actors responsible, and the impacts on victims. While this chapter in particular explores moral and political philosophy through Arendt's analysis, we would be remiss if we neglected how Arendt locates her work in the field of law, not psychology. That is, Arendt's construct of the *banality of evil* points to a larger legal problem, not simply a problem of the human psyche or moral core. The problem of the *banality of evil* exists in its inarticulability in law.

64 *Thoughtless and violence as work culture*

Felman (2002) explains:

> In describing Eichmann's borrowed (Nazi) language and his all-too-credible self-justification by the total absence of motives for the mass murder that he passionately carried out (lack of *mens rea*), Arendt's question is not, How can evil (Eichmann) be so banal? but, How can the banality of evil be addressed in legal terms and by legal means? On what new legal grounds can the law mete out the utmost punishment precisely to banality or to the lack of *mens rea*? How can the absence of *mens rea* in the execution of a genocide become itself the highest – and not just the newest – crime against humanity?
>
> (p. 108)

By *mens rea*, Felman and by extension Arendt are referring to the legal principle of a guilty mind, or the motive for a criminal act. Motive, or degrees of it, constitute an element to a crime alongside the act itself, and the severity of the crime tends to be measured by the severity of both the act and its intention. For example, first-degree murder is a more serious criminal offence than manslaughter, where seriousness is measured in proportion to the penalty and rests in the presence or absence of *mens rea*. What Arendt found so startling about the Eichmann trial was that there was no discernible motive for his actions, despite the act itself constituting the most serious criminal act a person could commit. How does law contend with an evil so banal, she wondered – an evil act so bereft of intent or reason given how thoughtlessly it was carried out?

Arendt's broader analysis of the Eichmann trial had to do with the problem it posed as an event of monumental historical import, as an event meant to construct monumental history. The Eichmann trial involved a long list of Holocaust survivors testifying to their experiences. Such a prosecutorial approach meant to hold responsible a singular offender for all the offences of the Holocaust. As the trial wore on, it became increasingly clear to Arendt that the offender on trial was terrifyingly ordinary, his role in the Holocaust revealing that, far from being a monster, he could have been anyone. His ordinariness thus undercut the historical purpose of the trial itself.

Arendt exchanged letters with her mentor Karl Jaspers, who urged her to be critical of the trial's broader moral or historical function. Jaspers advised: "we have to see these things in their total banality, in their prosaic triviality, because that's what truly characterizes them … I regard any hint of myth and legend with horror" (Arendt & Jaspers, 1946, p. 62). He cautioned, in other words, against interpreting the trial in poetic terms. Arendt agreed: "we have to combat all impulses to mythologize the horrible" (p. 51). Her analysis of the trial meant to strip it of its mythologizing affect. Once she had done so, she came to the conclusion that Eichmann was doomed to disappoint, because he was not inherently evil and thus not a person possessing a qualitative, constitutional difference that would mark him for the work of

Nazis. He was also, for Arendt, doomed to cast a shadow over the purpose of the trial itself – to make history, to hold a singular figure responsible for an evil regime– because the juridical nature of redress is meant to be far more circumscribed.

Felman (2002) characterizes Arendt's idea of justice as a "thoroughly ascetic, disciplined, conceptual experience, not an emotional stage for spectacular public expression" (p. 121). Law, as an exercise in measurement, structures and articulates transgressions, wrestles them into classifications for the purpose of finding resolutions. Law is thus a realm distanced from the Holocaust and other instances of mass violence, by nature of its function of finding a "basis for communication" (p. 151). On these grounds, Arendt was concerned over how the Eichmann trial transformed the courtroom into a space of theatre. Witnesses, for example, were selected and questioned in order to convey the scope of the Holocaust, rather than for their direct relation and relevance to Eichmann's actions. "This case," she critiqued, "was built on what the Jews had suffered, not on what Eichmann had done" (Arendt, 1963, p. 6). Therefore, for her, because the juridical function of the court was not properly carried out, the problem of the *banality of evil* – of the horrifying banality of his motive or lack thereof – was not properly addressed.

Arendt's resistance to the mythologizing impulse bears out in her critiques of witnesses, particularly K-Zetnik. A poet and Holocaust survivor, K-Zetnik was unable to give his name for testimony because in order to relate his experiences he had to relive the violence, particularly the dehumanizing force of being rendered nameless in concentration camp conditions. In the back and forth at trial over his name, and as his mind wandered back to traumatic memory, he fainted on the witness stand. Arendt "reserves some of her harshest language and some of the fiercest irony in *Eichmann in Jerusalem* for the description of K-Zetnik's unsuccessful court appearance" (Felman, 2002, p. 140) because in the eyes of the court, the witness testimony was inadmissible, and thus irrelevant to proceedings. He illustrated, for Arendt, the necessary limits of law, and the ways in which those limits were being tested in the Eichmann trial.

Perhaps some of these lessons are transferrable to the legal redress pursued in this new wave of deinstitutionalization politics. Patricia Seth and Marie Slark, the leading plaintiffs representing the class suing Ontario for negligence in managing the Huronia Regional Centre, registered their dissatisfaction with the settlement. First, they raised objections regarding the amount of compensation awarded and the handling of the claims process, indicating that the outcome did not feel like justice. But, perhaps more importantly, the let-down that a settlement precluded their "day in court," their use of the courtroom as a platform for recounting instances of injustice, revealed a certain sense of expectation around what can be accomplished in a legal setting. To this, Arendt might respond that the courtroom is a place of limits, and so it was bound to disappoint those who have a wider

66 *Thoughtless and violence as work culture*

conceptualization of justice in mind. And, indeed, avoiding a trial might have been the ideal outcome given that Ontario courtrooms would have imposed limits on witness selection and testimony that would have curtailed the narratives told.

Our analysis of Huronia and comparable institutions suggests that former staff and their family employed a mythologizing impulse themselves when interpreting the Institutional Cases and their surrounding activisms. That the law was tasked with contending with instances of abuse and the role of the state in perpetuating conditions for abuse is not negated by there being staff members who genuinely applied themselves to their jobs, or enjoyed their work, or followed protocol. That former residents of Schedule 1 facilities have experienced wrongdoing that qualifies them for financial compensation or a public apology is not negated by the affection staff felt for those in their care. That there was violence in institutions, and that institutionalization itself is a violence, does not render the people implicated evil, not inherently so. However, it *does* speak to a culture of thoughtlessness, a culture that discouraged judgment or empathic concern. It would appear that that culture outlives the institutions themselves whenever a staff member or their family reacts viscerally to survivor accounts, and refuses to demonstrate empathy.

While Arendt functioned as a useful framing device for making sense of staff members' lack of criticality, we depart from her legal analysis when she shows disdain for Holocaust witnesses, or at least their role in legal proceedings. We instead follow Felman in her more sympathetic reading of K-Zetnik, whose testimony "which defies at once legal reduction and legal closure, must remain unrealized, unfinished" (2002, p. 151). We avoid and dismantle cultures of violence by turning to survivors, by countenancing and contemplating their accounts, by finding value and meaning in K-Zetnik fainting. If the law is not a place for this sort of work, that may signal a failing in law; and, also, that law is but one tool for communicating about and responding to injustice.

5 Quantifying and re-inscribing violence

In 2010, survivors of institutional violence brought a landmark class action lawsuit against the Government of Ontario for failing in its fiduciary duty[1] in relation to the mistreatment of residents at the Huronia Regional Centre between 1945 and 2009. Plaintiffs Patricia Seth and Marie Slark and their litigation guardians Marilyn and Jim Dolmage insisted on legal recognition of and compensation for the intense suffering of residents residing at Huronia during this time-period. In 2013, a $35-million settlement was reached out of court. The settlement in many ways marks a victory and endeavours to simplify forms and instructions.[2] Nevertheless, the claims process has been marked by a sustained lack of attention to the engagement of legal discourse with notions of and assumptions around ability, and may be leaving out a great deal of what was experienced on the HRC site.

In this chapter, we identify the shortcomings found in the language and terms of the settlement, in order to lay the groundwork for alternative methods of raising consciousness and seeking reparation. We describe the settlement language not as a victory but rather as an extension of the failure of justice that marks Huronia's very fraught history. This history is violent, for the settlement directly addresses forms of physical and sexual abuse; we move beyond this truth to claim that practices of institutionalization are inherently and systemically violent. Further, the legal processes by which those practices are discursively framed – or even left out of analysis – themselves commit acts of violence in the particular ways in which they fail and disempower claimants. We ask: how does the language of the claims process work to re-inscribe systemic forms of injustice? To do so, we look first at the structure and language of the settlement and address ways in which the discourse employed may further marginalize the most vulnerable within the class and inadvertently retrench forms of trauma. Second, we explore how the language of the settlement extends harmful discursive institutional practices and may in fact leave open space for institutionalization to reoccur.

Understanding the language of the settlement

As noted in the Ontario Superior Court hearing during which the aggrieved parties were certified as a class,[3] the Huronia Regional Centre was opened

68 *Quantifying and re-inscribing violence*

under provincial statutory law, the 1839 *Act to authorize the erection of an Asylum within this Province for the reception of Insane and Lunatic persons*, and was sustained under subsequent statutes. Its primary goal was to contain individuals who fit within newly emerging (and eugenically informed) diagnostic criteria for what has been alternately termed idiocy, mental retardation, developmental and intellectual disability. At its height in the middle of the twentieth century, Huronia's major focus was housing and re-mediating children with intellectual disabilities, although there was always a wide age range among residents.

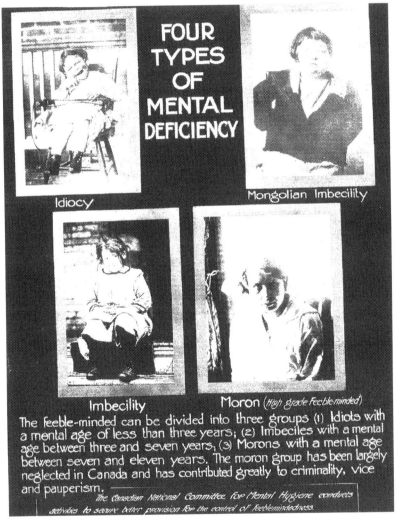

Figure 5.1 An undated Canadian eugenic-era educational leaflet describing and identifying four types of mental deficiencies.

Quantifying and re-inscribing violence 69

During the institution's tenure, as cited through the class certification process, the Crown received a 1971 report wherein Walton B. Williston identified staff shortages, overcrowding, outdated living residences, and coerced labour for little or no pay (*Dolmage v Ontario*, 2010, ONSC 1726). In the suit, plaintiffs alleged that the Crown failed in its duties to residents by ignoring report findings and keeping Huronia open for decades thereafter. This breach, they claimed, resulted in emotional, physical, and psychological abuse (*Dolmage v Ontario*, 2010, ONSC 1726). By 2013, allegations of a breach entailed more specifically the Crown's "funding, operation, management, administration, supervision and control of the Huronia Regional Centre" (*Dolmage v Ontario*, 2010, ONSC 6131, para. 29). The class alleged that the Crown failed to enact prevention policies or improve quality of care, notwithstanding reports like Williston's of overcrowding and understaffing, and recommendations for improvement.

Such were the arguments raised before a settlement was reached. The terms of the settlement were developed in consultation with disability advocacy groups and were heralded in the case law for reflecting "the sensitive nature of this litigation and the unique circumstances of the class members" (*Dolmage v HMQ*, 2013, para. 23). This was accomplished, in part, by providing non-monetary benefits: a formal apology; the production of case documents for scholarly research; and a number of commemorative initiatives, including a plaque, a registry, appropriate signage on the cemetery grounds, scheduled access to Huronia grounds, as well as an opportunity for scholars to archive artefacts (paras. 12–13). Further, a settlement fund was established that amounted to $35 million, in addition to costs to the Crown for administering the claims process, and the promise that compensation awards would not be subject to taxation or claw-backs (para. 13).

The settlement agreement entailed a system for determining eligibility for funds, demarcated by two claim forms. Section A claims for up to $2,000 required only a solemn declaration of harm while institutionalized at Huronia, without need of evidence or detail. Claimants were directed on the form to check a box indicating, "I was harmed or hurt when I lived at Huronia or at a place where Huronia put me" (Koskie Minksy LLP, 2015). Section B claims required details of harm or abuse in writing, and the amount of financial compensation awarded was based on the allocation of points for the amount of harm incurred at the institution. Within this document, claimants were instructed to identify harm or abuse, and were provided with a series of examples of actionable physical harms, including "calling you names, insulting or yelling at you;" "giving you scars, bruises, broken bones, broken teeth or any other injury to your body or how you look;" "giving you too much or too little, or the wrong medication" (pp. 9–10). Examples of sexual abuse included "touching or making you touch someone else in a sexual way when you did not want to;" "making you watch, listen or talk about sexual things when you do not

70 *Quantifying and re-inscribing violence*

want to;" "making you stand or walk around naked;" "putting or trying to put something in your mouth, vagina or anus when you did not want them to" (p. 11). The document stated after these lists, "there are many other things that are abuse," and directed claimants to "write down anything that harmed you" (p. 12).

The compensation scheme tasked Justice Ian Binnie with overseeing the claims administration process and, alongside Crawford Class Action Services, evaluating Section B claim forms and assigning points according to the settlement agreement's point allocation system (*Dolmage v HMQ*, 2013). Under the point allocation system, there were six possible categories of abuse. Under "physical assault," level one for 100 points consisted of repeated, persistent, and excessive wrongful acts – demeaning behaviour, humiliation, or physical punishment; level two for 200 points entailed assaults not resulting in serious physical injury; and level three for 400 points required that acts resulted in serious physical injury, such as a bruise or laceration. Level one sexual assaults – non-consensual behaviour or contact – constituted 200 points; level two, repeated non-consensual sexual behaviour, was worth 400 points; and level three, or repeated incidents of serious sexual assault amounted to 600 points. The number of points tallied on claims determined the amount of compensation awarded, up to $35,000 per Section B claimant (a maximum limit that could increase to $42,000 if Section B claims did not exhaust the net settlement fund) (*Dolmage v HMQ*, 2013).

Quantifying injustice: a critique of terminology and process

While the examples offered in the Section B claim form and the typology of abuse outlined in the point allocation system sound like adequate – indeed, striking – illustrations of violence, and certainly should be catalogued and accounted for, there is also much to critique about both the language and process of these claims. First, what is clear from the identified examples is an emphasis on *active* language. Throughout the proceedings, court justices cited the plaintiffs' allegations that the Crown was in breach of a duty of care resulting in HRC residents being actively harmed, as well as neglected to the point of harm (e.g., *Dolmage v Ontario*, 2010, ONSC 1726). However, settling out of court has meant that the most definitive and precise declaration that the Crown committed wrongdoing can be found in Premier of Ontario Kathleen Wynne's public apology, which directly addressed neglect as a form of harm;[4] and as the claims process unfolded, the Crown was not held accountable or required to compensate for harm born of institutional neglect, often resulting in grievous forms of abuse and mistreatment.

In settlement documents, particularly the claim forms themselves, "neglect" was left absent from claimable items. While the term 'neglect' might signal a range of possible scenarios that illustrate systemic issues within the

Quantifying and re-inscribing violence 71

institution – overcrowding, understaffing, lack of resources, lack of adequate training – the move to 'abuse' in the claim form denotes a much more active relationship to harm, i.e., the wilful and conscious – not systemic – inflicting of pain or suffering on another. Given this seemingly minor linguistic shift, some of the very important nuance to the harms experienced is lost, like when children spent the better part of their days in diapers and caged cribs because not enough staff were available to tend to them, or survivors had their teeth surgically removed after years of inadequate dental care. How does one account for regimens of approved medications that came with severe and lasting side effects; the instances where residents were seen nude simply because they lacked clean clothes or their bathroom stalls lacked doors; the number of years spent uneducated because education cost money and was thought wasted on the intellectually disabled; the exploited labour residents had to invest in maintaining their own prison because work cultivated moral character?

This linguistic shift is deeply problematic, especially for survivors at a significant disadvantage in terms of making or substantiating claims. First, survivors who are able to talk, struggle to define normal daily living practices *as forms of abuse*. Second, and perhaps more problematically, non-verbal survivors, survivors who cannot revisit their memories of violence without experiencing profound re-traumatization, and the dead (many of whom are buried in unmarked graves, their original tombstones dug up and repurposed for sidewalks on the HRC grounds) (Alamenciak, 2014) are left at a disadvantage because they cannot adequately or at all describe whether and how injuries or mistreatment occurred. Caregivers, support workers, and loved ones have been tasked with cobbling together reasonable explanations for possible harm relying on institutional and medical records, resultant behaviours (phobias, compulsions, often-repeated phrases, etc.), and accounts of other, verbal survivors who were residents at the same time. Given that instances of institutional abuse were rarely included as such within residents' files, much of the content of these claims is based on informed guesswork. There are also survivors who simply lack family support altogether when making claims. This means that the most egregious examples of violence may be identified, but more complicated instances of structural violence, even the structural conditions that make possible or exacerbate violence, are much more difficult to account for.

The harmful use of passive language and limiting survivors' capacity to articulate abuse and neglect is not novel to the claims process; indeed, these practices extend subtle but oppressive protocols which have roots within institutional histories. In her analysis of the oral history of Michener (an institution for intellectually disabled people in the province of Alberta, that parents and the state insist is humane to leave open, see CBC News, 2014), Malacrida (2015) observes that institutional case files use passive language to account for injury. Passive language fails to attribute injury to cause. Further, records of injury tend to appear only after family members visit

72 *Quantifying and re-inscribing violence*

and lodge complaints upon speaking with residents or witnessing bodily evidence of violence. She quotes case files:

> The files where evidence of violence was discussed are riddled with passive voice. For example, a resident injured by rough handling was described in language that almost sounds as if she injured herself: '[X] hit right eyebrow on bed rail while being put to bed sustaining a laceration'
>
> (p. 94)

Malacrida also discusses at length institutional strategies around isolating residents from the outside world by discouraging family from visiting, for the sake of facilitating adjustment; this would surely result in fewer complaints on record in the absence of advocates.

It is not unreasonable to assume similar practices were carried out at Huronia. The 1960 informational video about provincial institutions, *One on Every Street*, noted that family members of Huronia residents were advised by staff not to visit, when doing so negatively impacted residents' adjustment to institutional life. Located far from urban centres such as Toronto, Huronia was difficult to access and family members were permitted only to visit with residents in public spaces (i.e., common rooms) and for limited amounts of time. Parental access to spaces of deep neglect – overcrowded wards, for example – was not permitted. Thus, in the face of scant evidence, some HRC claimants were only capable of submitting Section A claim forms when they could have qualified for much more compensation than Section A claims can merit. Similarly, some claimants who submitted Section B claims were only able to supply limited testimony and have had their claims either downgraded to an "A" claim, or have received fewer points based on lack of clear evidence of active harm. This is particularly egregious with respect to highly impaired, non-verbal survivors who often had much longer institutional stays than more verbal survivors, and who would thus have undoubtedly witnessed abuse and neglect for very sustained periods of time – entire lifetimes, in some cases.

The logic of 'A few bad apples': leaving space for institutionalization

The work to recount Huronia has begun in the courtroom. To quote Justice Barbara A. Conway's 2014 decision to approve class counsel's fees: "these class actions provided a means for [survivors] to … create public awareness of the history of these institutions and the alleged experiences of the residents there" (*Dolmage, McKillop and Bechard v HMQ*, 2014, para. 10). Certainly, HRC survivors should be heralded as legal trailblazers. However, legal victory has not meant justice – or rather, to equate legal victory with justice in this circumstance may mean that the conditions for institutional violence are not adequately challenged. Rather, given the limits of what tort

Quantifying and re-inscribing violence 73

law can accomplish,[5] this legal victory has involved the hierarchicalization and monetization of trauma, a weighing of the worth of trauma. Lost in the quantification of harm are the institutional dynamics and conditions that caused such harm, which cannot be quantified or even reasonably captured in the framework of legal storytelling. In leaving absent these conditions, the settlement problematically leaves open the possibility for institutionalization to reoccur.

A 2000 Law Commission of Canada (LCC) report on physical and sexual child abuse in Canadian institutional settings, including training schools for intellectually disabled youth, long-term mental health care facilities, and sanatoria (Law Commission of Canada, 2000), notes that turning to legal recourses for the purpose of redress – looking to the criminal justice system and pursuing lawsuits in civil court to hold people and government bodies responsible – reveals the limits to these systems to address systemic oppression. The report indicates in its analysis of criminal proceedings, and by extension civil proceedings:[6] "the criminal justice system is well-suited to identifying individual perpetrators of abuse and holding them liable. It is, however, less effective in shedding light on the systemic problems that may have allowed the abuse to occur in the first place" (p. 5). Ben-Moshe (2014) seems to agree with this assessment, arguing that justice frameworks of this sort fail to "address the structural inequalities that lead to injustice in the first place [or to] question the basic assumptions of the system" (p. 260). Her recommendation is not reform but abolition of disability incarceration in all its manifestations, in order to go "beyond protesting the current circumstances, to creating new conditions of possibility by collectively contesting the status quo" (p. 256). This call for abolition is especially resonant given that, despite the rash of lawsuits following the HRC settlement, Alberta's Michener – the same Michener whose history is laid bare in Malacrida's work – remains open.

Thus, Huronia's history as recounted within the existing legal framework is fragmented, formal, missing pieces and accounts from the most vulnerable and least able to self-advocate, and may well be losing track of the experience of injustice through efforts to articulate it. The implications of this void are enormous, even beyond the problems around ensuring those wronged are compensated: that only abuse is acknowledged in the HRC claims process might imply that institutionalization can still be done right, with enough sensitivity, training, oversight, etc.; that is, that the problem lies with a few abusive 'bad apple' staff. The settlement language, with its emphasis on abuse rather than neglect, obfuscates institutional practices and dehumanizing forms of structural oppression inherent to institutionalization itself.

Given that institutional practices have, since their origins, created and perpetuated systemic violence, it is difficult to imagine what institutionalization 'done right' would entail. Asylums marked for treating mental retardation first established under the 1839 Ontario legislation were justified through segregationist, custodial policies and practices designed for the dual purpose of caring for people believed incapable of social integration and

74 *Quantifying and re-inscribing violence*

protecting communities from the multiple threats disability might pose – to safety, to reproduction, to social order. Rossiter and Clarkson (2013) claim in their socio-historical accounting of the HRC: "from their inception, life within Canadian institutions was unrelentingly oppressive [and] after many years of financial strain, provincial neglect, chronic overcrowding and prevailing cultural attitudes of fear, abjection and the need for social isolation left people with [intellectual disability diagnoses] in institutions vulnerable to widespread abuse" (p. 12). That is, abuse was made possible and routinized through systemic conditions. Stenfert Kroese and Holmes (2013) elaborate on these conditions, focusing on an historical trend to medicalize disability, or to categorize disability as a condition in need of fixing or curing in order to restore a person's health or species-typical status. The implications for persons labelled with "incurable" disabilities entail indefinite confinement and a social stigma impossible to overcome: "as there are no cures for learning disabilities,[7] patients were destined to stay in hospital until death. They were at the mercy of strict rules, regulations and routines whereby other people decided when they were to get up, when to wash, when to eat, what to wear, and who to befriend" (p. 71). Stenfert Kroese and Holmes go on to argue that extreme conditions of isolation, control, and deprivation have their impact upon persons, creating resistant behaviours, what the authors call severe psychological disturbances, and learned helplessness that through cyclical logic only serve to reinforce the call to keep those institutionalized out of communities and within carceral spaces (p. 71).

Canadian advocacy and self-advocacy organizations[8] have for these reasons supported deinstitutionalization. Adopted by the Canadian Association for Community Living, People First Canada, and Community Living Ontario in 2013, and endorsed by organizations across Canada, a document entitled "Common Principles on the Inclusion of People with Disabilities in their Communities" uses United Nations language to acknowledge "the physical, psychological and emotional harm people with disabilities have had to endure as a direct result of having been confined or forced to live in institutional settings" (BakerLaw, 2014). The principles endorsed in this document hold that institutions deny full citizenship and community inclusion, and *"do not and cannot* contribute to the health and well being of persons with disabilities" (emphasis our own, p. 2). People First Canada and the Canadian Association for Community Living have endeavored to realize these principles by monitoring progress toward deinstitutionalization in *Institution Watch*, a regular newsletter dedicated to the idea that "as a society, we have long ago recognized that institutions are just not good for people" (Larson & Haddad, 2016, p. 1).

Conclusions

Huronia's is a long yet living history that has yet to be responsibly documented. Persons housed there were relegated to a geographical and socio-political periphery, sometimes forgotten by loved ones, surely ignored by the state even when reports like Williston's surfaced. Their fiduciaries managed their stories – for persons diagnosed with intellectual disabilities are not always trusted to be authorities over their own experience. And, in institutional spaces like the HRC, acts of defiance, even the identification of wrongdoing, could result in punishment and medication. This is a reality that Seth and Slark experienced and related in their statements of claim:[9] Slark was medicated for "acting out," Seth, for "speaking out" (*Dolmage v Ontario*, 2010, ONSC 1726, paras. 29, 31). That this history lives on in now-aging survivors makes the task of recounting a history of injustice all the more pressing.

So, what is to be done about bearing witness to the suffering endured at the HRC? How do we account for histories that cannot be verbalized, trauma that cannot (and should not) be weighed through a system of points? We suggest that the settlement is best viewed as a starting point rather than a final victory. After all, to quote Urban Walker: "reparations can only ever be an act or process at one time; the reciprocal accountability they token must be secured and shown real over time" (2014, p. 129). That time, we argue, is just beginning for Huronia survivors, and the legal settlement offers an opportunity for reflection in order to better grasp the enormity of suffering, and to act on the knowledge that institutionalization is inherently violent. While we cannot predict where such reflection might lead, nor can we prescribe a remedy for those who must live with the ongoing consequence of institutional trauma, we can offer suggestions from our own experience regarding the potential role of the legal system as responsible parties in the work of collective memory-making around and beyond the HRC settlement.

The Law Commission of Canada report (2000) offers legally entrenched recommendations beyond civil proceedings. These include petitioning to Ombudsman offices, which are independent, impartial bodies appointed in their jurisdictions to investigate complaints and publicly report their policy recommendations to government. Similarly, public inquiries can offer recommendations for corrective action and are, according to the LCC report, "most effective in holding organizations and governments, not individuals, accountable for their actions" (p. 7). Truth and reconciliation commissions, like that which was organized for Indigenous populations subjected to residential schooling, are effective in cases of intergenerational injury that reverberate through communities. Beyond these recourses, the report recommends community initiatives for meeting "the most compelling needs of survivors by involving them directly in the design and delivery of helping and healing" (p. 8); and redress programs designed to meet survivors' needs through financial compensation and support.

Community initiatives have already developed around political action and community arts praxis. The organization *Remember Every Name* is known for its political activism related to the HRC cemetery, insofar as self-advocates and allies have been painstakingly working to document who is buried where (Alamenciak, 2014). *Tangled Art + Disability* has hosted an arts

76 *Quantifying and re-inscribing violence*

show, *Surviving Huronia*, where Seth and Slark told stories in their opening address, and art featuring themes of institutional life and violence were exhibited (Surviving Huronia, 2014). Also, our own collective *Recounting Huronia* has been working with survivors to story their experiences of institutionalization. These collectives have sought to honour the polyvocality of the survivor community, to respect and witness a wide variety of institutional experiences (however these may be expressed), and to build up community around, among, and with survivors, where social memory may be woven together, may come to be embodied and enfleshed, and may be shared in ways that are not easily ignored, dismissed, or forgotten. We believe these more flexible and nimble approaches may be better suited to the healing and activism vital in the search for justice for the Huronia survivor community.

Notes

1 A fiduciary duty is a legal term denoting an important relationship involving trust, where one party has power and the other party is vulnerable. Canadian law has marked physician/patient relationships as fiduciary in nature, for instance.
2 Retired Supreme Court Justice Ian Binnie and the Koskie Minsky law firm oversaw the claims process and, following a court mandate, ensured forms were in plain language. Slark and Seth also participated in efforts to tour Ontario community living centres, to teach survivors how to submit claims. The process was simplified to ensure persons with intellectual disabilities would not struggle with accessing compensation.
3 Class certification is a process according to which a group of people is found to share similar legal issues, so determination of the issues individuals raise is binding for the group. Class action lawsuits are brought under civil law, where an aggrieved party – in this case, a class of persons – can seek compensation from another party accused of committing wrongdoing that caused harm.
4 "In the case of Huronia, some residents suffered neglect and abuse within the very system that was meant to provide them care." *Ontario's Apology to Former Residents of Regional Centres for People with Developmental Disabilities*, delivered by Premier Kathleen Wynne (2013).
5 Tort law is an area of civil law where plaintiffs may sue for injuries or harms sustained due to some breach in duties owed.
6 Granted, civil proceedings include the mechanisms to solidify those wronged as a class, as well as the means to hold larger bodies – not just singular persons – accountable for wrongdoing. Nevertheless, as is the case in criminal proceedings, fault for active, overt instances of wrongdoing is certainly easier to find than systemic or structural oppression that is diffuse, generational, and woven into social fabrics.
7 Stenfert Kroese and Holmes are discussing institutionalization in the UK context, where the term learning disability is equivalent to the North American term intellectual or developmental disability.
8 Self-advocates and self-advocacy organizations distinguish their work (hence the term *self*-advocacy) from advocacy efforts conducted on their behalf (led by service providers, parents, and persons with physical disabilities).
9 Plaintiffs begin civil proceedings by filing statements of claim that outline the reasons for pursuing a lawsuit. Defendants receive statements of claim in order to prepare their response, and courts refer to these documents when determining whether the case should proceed.

6 Embedded trauma and embodied resistance

Connie stands at the microphone. Her small, hunched frame stands steady, with hands gripping her walker. Her thin, blond-grey hair falls like a veil over eyes scrunched tightly shut. *"YOU HURT MEEEEEEEEEE,"* she wails. *"I HATE YOU."* The sound rumbles like an earthquake through the room. The floor shakes and trembles. The windows chatter like teeth. We hold the shuddering walls. The sound moves through our bodies, rides our limbs. We hold the sound; the sound overtakes us. It is fundamental and unstoppable, like a natural disaster.

We are at the Huronia Regional Centre site, which has been opened to the public for one final weekend in 2014 before being permanently closed. Tours of the institution are being run by officious young government employees who carry clipboards and wear purple shirts that read "staff," like camp counsellors. We are here with a group of people who know Huronia with painful intimacy – institutional survivors who lived at this site for years, even decades. It is these survivors who can tell you what it was like to be kept in solitary confinement wearing a strait jacket you had been forced to sew yourself. These survivors can show you around the morgue where they were forced to clean bodies, can tell you about being forced to parade naked around the euphemistically-named "playroom," can tell you where they were hit and fondled, ignored and berated.

We have also brought a team of artists to secretly intervene on the space before it closes. Sound artists Christof Migone and Marla Hlady have managed to sneak cartloads of industrial sound equipment past the prying eyes of the government tour guides and have located themselves in the former "playroom" of the girls' ward, where many of our survivor colleagues experienced routine physical and sexual abuse. In this room, now barren save for mint-green walls and cracked linoleum, Migone and Hlady have placed a single microphone attached to several enormous speakers, which they have screwed into the walls and doors. Using their equipment, Migone and Hlady amplify and distort sounds made into the microphone, and these sounds travel directly through the speakers, literally into the walls of the institution (see Hlady & Migone, 2017).

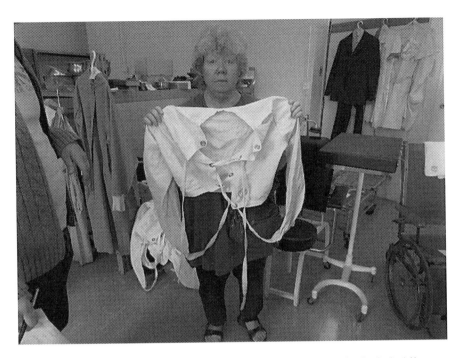

Figure 6.1 Huronia class action lawsuit lead Plaintiff Patricia Seth holding an adult-sized strait jacket, taken at the institution following its closure.
Photographer nancy viva davis halifax.

Figure 6.2 A dilapidated former "playroom" at the Huronia Regional Centre. Survivors describe hours of monotony punctuated with episodes of violence occurring in these spaces.
Photographer Jen Rinaldi.

Embedded trauma, embodied resistance 79

Our survivor colleagues are invited to speak to the building – the edifice that housed so much of their pain and suffering. Some tell stories. Some speak directly to abusers. Others simply make noise: wails, grunts, moans. Every noise, every resonant sound has an impact on the building, moves the site. Every word has an impact. "We shook the walls," they say with awe as they step from the microphone. "We made it move."

French philosopher and literary theorist, Roland Barthes (1977), writes that the "grain" of the voice is the "materiality of the body speaking its mother tongue" (p. 182). This is to say that the voice is a product, a trace, a remnant of an embodied self. In this way, the survivors' embodied experiences of pain and suffering literally returned to shake the site where they were so deeply harmed. Survivor voices, in this sense, had a real, tangible, physical impact on the world around them – rattling the foundations of the building that contained their pain.

In this final chapter we explore what it means to survive institutional violence. While the lasting impact of violence and trauma is both clear and unassailable, the question of what it means to survive institutional violence, which is rooted in particular bureaucratic and organizational structures, is more complicated. What does institutional survivorship look like over a lifetime, long after the walls of the institution cease to confine? How does the logic of institutional organization reproduce itself in and through individuals over a lifetime, and how do survivors rally agency and bravery to resist the long reach of the institution?

This chapter examines both how the logic of institutional organization exerts itself over a lifetime in and through embodied experience, as well as the ways in which institutional survivors resist this replication, assert agency, and live bravely against the chronic pull of institutionalization. We look at instances in which survivors reproduce forms of institutional organization in their daily lives outside the institution. Institutionalization, we argue, is a *logic* rather than a *space* and, in this sense, inescapable. However, bound up in the drive to reproduce damaging and violent forms are crucial points of *resistance* and *resilience* – moments when survivors preserve bodily agency and integrity, protect their right to pleasure and satisfaction, provide care for others even in the face of the profound neglect, reach across loneliness to find connection, and refashion trauma into bravery. Survivorship, in this sense, means more than simply living through the experience of institutionalization: it is the determined work of claiming whole, complicated personhood against and despite the eradicative and reductive force of the institution-within.

To mount this argument, we rely on ethnographic observation compiled over four years of working with and alongside Huronia survivors. We use a self-consciously interpretive analytic framework through which to reimagine small moments of psychic and bodily force as instances of embodied reproduction of, and resistance to, the logic of institutionalization. While our group focused directly on issues of institutionalization, relying

80 *Embedded trauma, embodied resistance*

on workshop focus groups and in-depth interviews as a means to help survivors describe and articulate their memories and lived experiences of Huronia, as researchers we also spent a great deal of time observing the survivors in their present daily lives. Our roles as researchers extended well past the structured 'research' time allotted to the project, allowing us to form rich and complicated relationships with our survivor colleagues. We spent time with survivors and their family members, visited their homes, shared meals, travelled together to conferences and workshops and site visits. We went to court together. We talked together on the phone, on Facebook, via text message. These observations, then, are impartial and biased, inflected by the weight of improbable friendships formed through the crucible of emancipatory and participatory research. These observations are made from a place of deep respect and an unabating sense of the injustices that are continually perpetuated against our survivor colleagues. This is to say that these observations are our own, but made in the service of upholding survivor integrity.

Theoretical framework

The body has become a topic of increasing, explicit importance as a theoretical focus, in particular the sociology of health and illness and disability studies. Shilling (1993) notes that the body was an "absent presence" within classical sociological thinking, haunted by the spectre of the Cartesian mind/body split. Our scholarship may be so absent consideration of the body due to how bodily processes – the mechanisms of perception, internal system functioning – tend to "recede into the corporeal background" (Gimlin, 2006, p. 701). Indeed, body appears in health and disability scholarship precisely because health conditions and disability diagnoses are marked as moments of corporeal disruption, moments when the body forces itself into focus as a problem (Shildrick, 1997). Scholarship working to overcome early conceptual neglect has been organized around understanding the 'problem' of the body from multiple perspectives, in particular the relation of the body to selfhood (Shilling, 1993, 1997), the workings of power and social relations (Foucault, 1979), and ontological disposition (Turner, 1992).

Scholarship of this sort points to how identity is necessarily embodied. Goffman's work offers a nuanced discussion regarding identity, including the individual and collective 'construction' and 'reconstruction' of 'reality' through the imputation of meaning. Goffman (1963) looks specifically at the processes by which "deviants," or those who fall outside an accepted social norm, are separated or marked as "culturally unacceptable" (Williams, 1987, p. 136) through social interaction. He highlights "the force a stigmatizing label and the attendant stereotypical beliefs and attitudes can have upon an individual's sense of identity and being" (Williams, 1987, p. 138). This work provides a nuanced analysis of types of stigma, the constitutive effects of stigma on identity, and the ways that those facing stigma manage their identity, presentation of self, and social interactions, all of which are inevitably fraught with anxiety and tension due to the presence of difference and abnormality.

Of interest here are observations regarding the social form of stigma. These include: stigma's ability to radiate "in waves" (Goffman, 1963) from the stigmatized individual to family and community members; "interactional, adaptive strategies" (Williams, 1987, p. 142) utilized by stigmatized individuals such as "passing" (as normal) and "covering" (the difference) to *manage* tension; and, the profound effects that these efforts have on the stigmatized. Here, links between stigma and identity take place through the body, and the management of bodily interactions. Shilling (1993) flags the importance of the body in both structuring and mediating between social encounter and identity. It is the body's inability to perform social roles with competence or "poise" that leads to embarrassment, but it is also the body that communicates these failures through a sense of incompetence and discomfort (p. 86). This sense of embarrassment not only leads to a reconfiguration of identity as "discredited" (Goffman, 1963), but also necessitates embodied management strategies on the part of the stigmatized. Shilling (1993) writes: "the body assumes the status of a resource which can be managed in a variety of ways in order to construct a particular version of the self" (p. 74). Here, we are looking not at embodied stigma itself, but rather, embodied strategies to undo stigma, to challenge and resist the kinds of discredited identities created through the experience of institutionalization.

Goffman's contemporary and a leading scholar on institutionalization and embodiment, Foucault is particularly relevant to discourse on bodily production and resistance. Foucault (1979) articulates a theory of biopower, or the strategies and arrangements of state designed for the administration of populations. For Foucault, power is diffuse in macro- and micro-political relations – not a resource or a tangible thing, but an enactment that transpires between persons or collectives. Specifically, biopower is deployed, overinvested (Cohen, 2009) in the areas of life, health, and hygiene, taking the forms of "regulatory and corrective mechanisms" (Foucault, 1978, p. 144; see also Drinkwater, 2015). These correctives, these disciplinary activities, comprise instruments, techniques, and procedures that take as their objective the production of "subjected and practiced bodies, 'docile bodies'" (Foucault, 1979, p. 137). The target of biopower is the body, its capacities and potentialities and transgressions. Biopower works on, in, and through bodies to transform and improve them, to contain and control them: "The human body [enters] a machinery of power that explores it, breaks it down and rearranges it" (p. 138). But Foucault's model is not deterministic, given that not all bodies are ground down to the point of docility. He holds that power is not just repressive, but also productive; and not only centralized in the state, but so diffuse it can be reorganized. So, there exist in this constellation of power arrangements, strategies of resistance.

82 Embedded trauma, embodied resistance

Relatedly, gender theorist and philosopher, Judith Butler (1990), theorizes the concept of *performativity* and in so doing re-imagines subjectivity as fluid rather than fixed. In particular, Butler is concerned with understanding the ways in which particular identities (gender, race, or disability, for example) are not a pre-given, ontological truth, but rather a *process,* whereby we are called (and call ourselves) into certain types of being. Fraser and Greco (2005) describe the centrality of the material body to Butler's project in the following manner:

> [The material body] does not 'exist' in and of itself, for *all* time, but is instead repeatedly produced *over* time through *performativity (performativity is that which brings into being or enacts what it names)...* The subject may appear to have 'an identity', an identity which is resolutely written on the body, but this is only because reiteration 'conceals or dissimulates the conventions of which it is a repetition'.
>
> (pp. 45–46)

Thus, for Butler, both the body and its performativity are key to understanding subject formation, for it is the body's (performative) repetition of discourse and discursive practice that simultaneously creates an understanding of the subject and the body itself.

It is in this relationship between discourse and performative bodily acts ("performatives") and identities that Butler (1990) sees spaces for *resistance* to these same dominant discourses. Far from dictating the body's every move (and thus a sense of identity itself), discourse can be subverted and countered by the performative body. Performatives are often "indeterminate," that is, marginalized, "abnormal" bodies may perform in opposition to, or in challenge of, the discourses that call them into marginalization and abnormality. In our work, we explore the performative bodily work that survivors undertake in order to disrupt and resist dominant (and often shaming) social discourses regarding disability.

This seminal theory-work on embodiment has been liberally applied in disability studies (e.g., Mitchell & Snyder, 2015; Tremain, 2015), especially in relation to institutionalization. Malacrida's (2015) analysis of practices common to Alberta's Michener Centre is informed by Foucauldian theory, for instance, particularly Foucault's interest in how spatial arrangements and ritualized practices in prisons and asylums produce power relations to manage daily life: "this use of space to monitor large congregations of docile bodies is a hallmark of modern disciplinary societies" (p. 68). Dyck (2013) draws on Goffman and Foucault when exploring the diaries of Doreen Befus, survivor of the Michener Centre. Dyck notes how Doreen emphasizes her performance of daily activities like cooking, cleaning, and church, and suggests that these diaries reflect an extension of the institutional surveillance to which Doreen had grown accustomed: "her every move and utterance had been subject to scrutiny in the institution; now, left to her own devices,

Doreen remained constantly prepared for external judgment" (p. 154). And yet, both Malacrida and Dyck show in their respective analyses of survivor testimony that there exist and develop pockets of push-back against systems of power. These scholars reveal strategies of survival, negotiation, and resistance – active engagement with the machinery of the institution – during and after institutionalization. Here, we seek to extend the analysis, to show how institutional violence as an expression of biopower left lasting impressions on survivors' bodies, and – importantly – how survivors interpreted institutional violence and illustrated resistance through corporeal performativity.

Hair hygiene: discipline and rebellion

Pam's grey wiry hair is short – an inch or two at most. She cuts it herself, almost obsessively. She tells me that she stands at the mirror and lops off her curly locks as soon as they are "too long." She loves long hair, she tells me. She touches my hair sometimes – "beautiful," she says. Beautiful. But, still, her own hair is a different matter. When she was at the institution, she had to line up with the other girls. The staff berated her, told her that her hair was unruly, forced her to sleep in uncomfortable rollers every night. She despairs at the memory. Nothing she did managed to make her hair acceptable. Her hair needed to look like everyone else's. "I had fuzzy curly hair. It was really, really fuzzy. It looked like I stuck my finger in a light socket," Pam tells me. She tells me that she hated it. That she got picked on. That she still hates her hair – that it sticks out all over the place and that it does not grow properly.

A central organizational trait that contributed to institutional violence had to do with the Institution's overriding goal of reforming or refashioning residents into a malleable, docile, and uniform population. This often occurred through demands in and on the body. Institution staff forced residents to dress alike, sleep *en masse*, eat the same food at the same time, move from one place to another as a singular entity – a single-file line up. Individuality thus ceded to the demand for uniformity – or so implied the logic of the institution – and bound up in this demand was an underlying reliance on violence as a means to produce uniformity and conformity. Often, examples of the institution's demand for resident reformation occurred through small, seemingly incidental incidences of bodily incursion – like accusing Pam of slovenly hair care and forcing her to sleep in uncomfortable rollers.

Pam's response to this relatively minor command is telling in multiple directions. First, the reach of institutional norms for Pam is far longer than her actual time in the institution. Decades following her release from Huronia, Pam is still haunted by the fear of humiliation, still feels deeply the demand to 'fix' her hair, still bristles at the injustice of both the accusation (of not having brushed her hair) and the punishment (sleeping in painful rollers; being made fun of publicly). Her hair is a source of worry, marks her as

84 *Embedded trauma, embodied resistance*

different and therefore at risk of punishment. But at the same time, Pam's response to this internalized accusation and demand is both angry and liberatory. Yes, she is acquiescing to the internal call that her hair not be "messy all the time," but she does so in a way that is distinctly contrary to the demand placed by the institution, which was for women residents to be neat and feminine. Rather, Pam takes matters into her own hands, resists this call and cuts her own hair as short as she can, choosing to sport a masculine, neat haircut.

Conversely, Brian's hair is a beautiful sheet of silver-white that falls past his shoulders, straight and clean. Brian sports a rugged type of masculinity: he is a solid man who is good with his hands and wears lumberjack shirts and drives a pick-up truck. The hair, then, feels somehow anomalous, rebellious. Brian tells me (Kate) that he does not trust men with short hair; the men who hurt him at Huronia sported short hair, as was the style in the 1950s and '60s. He tells me about the doctor at Huronia: "he was one of the guys that put his hands on me." I ask him to tell me more about this, and he expounds:

> I was thrown down some stairs went there and they, they banged me up. And then I remember [the doctor] – he used to put his hands down my pants. He used to wear glasses, too. I remember really short hair, like, I mean short hair. …He was a tall, uh when you're a kid your tall uh any adults are tall to ya.

Brian tells me that he will never forget, and will be forever vigilant:

> [I'm] just cautious now. Uh I can't be in the same place where anybody's got really short hair. Like you know that crewcut they used to wear way back in the '60s? I can't be [in] a room where a guy [has this haircut], I won't.

At the same time that Brian was being abused by staff, he was also forced to emulate their appearance, at least superficially, as he and the other boys had their heads compulsorily shaved. This, Brian thinks in retrospect, had to do with managing a large and overcrowded population of bodies. I ask about having his hair forcibly shaved and Brian tells me, laughing ruefully: "you didn't have a choice. You sat in a chair, they shaved ya bald. You didn't have a choice whatsoever, 'cause I understand it now. I didn't then: Head lice."

Brian tells me he hasn't had short hair in years. The efforts of the institution to refashion him persist and haunt him. While he now feels that he understands the institutional rationale for shaving boys' heads, this seems to matter very little given the ways in which this forced him to both comply with the institutional demand for uniformity and to identify with the older men who abused him. Of course, the choice to shave boys' heads is not just a matter of bodily management; it is entirely bound up with expressions of masculinity. The girls, who would have been just as likely to have lice as the boys, were made to wear longer hair, which, as Pam recounts, demanded other forms of conformity and management. Rather, shaving the boys' heads erased traces of embodied individuality with the aim of turning unruly subjects into compliant objects, each the same as the next.

Brian evades the long reach of this practice, resists the pull back to institutional conformity by growing his hair long, by refusing to engage with people sporting crewcuts. He chooses, but he also does not choose; growing his hair seems conscious but somehow involuntary – like any other choice would be an unbearable embodiment of that which he seeks to resist and forget.

Mealtimes: chronic deprivation and demanding more

James's caregiver spoons mush into his mouth. She moves the utensil from the cup to his lips with deliberation, watching for his cues: has he swallowed; does his mouth open, bird-like, for more? She wipes his lips, pauses, begins again with a careful methodical pace. James was institutionalized by the time he was four years old, following his diagnosis of Down syndrome. Now 65, he has lived in a group home with two other men for almost their whole lives. All of his food must be blended into paste because he lacks teeth, and thickened because he eats so quickly; he bolts his food and aspirates, causing him to become sick. When asked about his habits, his workers tend to sigh that they cannot get James to stop eating so quickly – they cannot prevent this quirk. But his housemates share the same habit. *This is institutional muscle memory.* While they now live in a comfortable and quiet house, with ample time to eat and workers who take care to notice what they like and dislike, all three men share in common the history of living in a place where mealtime was short and chaotic.

James does not have the words to describe mealtime at the institution, but others fill in details. Stanely explains:

> If I didn't eat breakfast, then I don't get anything until lunch. If I don't eat lunch, it's the same at supper. If you don't eat supper, you don't get anything even in the night until breakfast the next day.

In short, meals were an instance when the logics of *austerity* and *deprivation* operated as overriding institutional ideologies. Here, we mean austerity and deprivation in a broad sense; institutions such as Huronia did not necessarily deprive residents of food itself (although for some who were deemed overweight or who were punished for other reasons, this was certainly the case) but rather denied residents the *pleasure* of food, the *pleasure* of eating. Receiving food, being fed, feeding, and eating entail basic forms of care, nourishment, enjoyment, and autonomy. In an institutional setting, eating is reduced to an act of population management: filling residents with the minimal amount of

86 *Embedded trauma, embodied resistance*

calories in a convenient and efficient manner. Mealtime, for example, was limited. The food, which was often bland, monotonous, and composed of cheap ingredients, was not meant to be savoured. David describes:

> I remember the food was bland. Uhm as far as meal times uh just, I just remember uh the end there, doing the same thing and eating your dinner or your breakfast or your lunch and filing down and filing back and you didn't really go anywhere else. I remember when you go down you're, you're against the wall, all the windows and file down to the left of the servery and get your stuff and sit down and eat.

Residents sat at large tables while staff patrolled the eating areas. Food had to be eaten quickly before mealtime ended, and to avoid someone else grabbing your portion.

And, so, James – like his housemates – continues to consume his food at an aggressively fast pace. This is particularly true of foods he likes: birthday cake, soda, chocolate bars. While the habit is clearly detrimental to his health, it is also important to read into this act a note of resistance and self-care. Driven by the logic of austerity, the institution certainly could not be counted on to protect or honour residents' need for pleasure and satisfaction in terms of food. Therefore, residents had to develop strategies to satisfy their own desires and to meet their own emotional needs. Rapid food consumption can thus be seen as a method of self-preservation and control of one's enjoyment and desire. It is, then, particularly ironic and heart breaking that, despite living in a home where his gustatory pleasure and desire finally stand a chance of being acknowledged by his caregivers, his ability to eat freely has been so deeply limited by his ongoing health concerns.

We came to understand the importance of food as a means of combating an embodied ethos of austerity in our workshops. Our survivor-colleagues travel a long way to participate in our workshops, so providing a meal ensures no one is hungry during our sessions. From a material perspective, we have understood from the outset that deprivation and austerity continue in very real ways outside the walls of the institution. Some of our survivor-colleagues live in poverty or near-poverty. Many rely on different forms of public assistance to get by, including disability pensions, food banks, and public housing. Early institutional life all but assured a life of chronic deprivation and need, particularly for those who did not have a family support system outside the institution. Individuals who were independent enough to live on their own after leaving the institution did so without the skills training or educational attainment to make an adequate living in mainstream society.

What we anticipated less was the emotional importance of eating together and providing certain kinds of foods for our survivor-colleagues, made clear

Embedded trauma, embodied resistance 87

through a litany of demands and involved discussion around what to order, from which restaurant, how food is prepared. It has been important, for example, that we have more than enough food on hand to ensure that no one feels shy about eating as much as they would like. Some survivor-colleagues have very strong feelings about what kind of food we order, making insistent requests about which pizza toppings come on the pizza, or vociferously complaining when we have eaten pizza too often, preferring that we switch our take-out orders. We also use our workshop time to celebrate with food, making sure to bring homemade cake to every meeting in order to sing happy birthday or mark other major milestones. There are always requests about which kind of cake we should have. There are never leftovers; if food remains, it is meticulously collected up in makeshift containers for survivor-colleagues to take home.

Sometimes, their insistence regarding what foods we eat felt burdensome – our group is large and there are many requests to accommodate. However, behind those requests lies a self-protective and resistant insistence on preserving pleasure, on demanding recognition for individual tastes and desires. Certainly, after years of taking what they were offered at institutional mealtimes, it might be expected that survivors would have learned not to complain, not to ask for more, not to expect anything from the transaction of being fed. But rather than acquiesce to the institution's demand to strip pleasure and satisfaction from food, our survivor-colleagues rightfully push for something different. Food in our workshops is an act of love, an act of recognition, an act of redress for injustice – past and present, material and emotional – and we make sure there is enough.

Pet care: imposed isolation and managing loneliness

Connie has had two children, one of whom was fathered by a staff member of the institution. She lost both: one died, the other removed to custodial care by the state. She had a husband, but he too died. She lives alone and struggles with a history of abuse so profound it scarcely seems believable. Despite this fraught relationship to isolation, Connie understands herself as someone who is an adept caretaker. She loves animals, so much so that she tells me people called her St. Francis when she was young. She has had a succession of black cats named Midnight, to "keep evil away." Some of her cats have needed intense and specialized forms of medical intervention.

Midnight the Third was diabetic and required absolutely regular meal times, special food, and insulin injections. Connie planned her days around Midnight's special needs, making sure to rise at particular times, feed him an approved diet, and return home when he needed his multiple medications. Connie understood this relationship as one of mutual reliance and caregiving. She talked about how much she and Midnight

88   *Embedded trauma, embodied resistance*

depended on one another; she to provide food, care, and love, and he to provide stability and a sense of calm when she was overcome with traumatic flashbacks. Indeed, when Connie had a traumatic dissociation during an early workshop, visualizing Midnight cradled in her arms calmed her immeasurably. Connie also attributed Midnight with a particular *spiritual* force: she imagined Midnight as a kind of guardian angel who would, in her fantasy, claw the eyes out of her tormentors, would tell her abusers to "leave his mummy alone."

Like Connie, Margaret has a complicated relationship with the twinned forces of isolation and caregiving. Like many "high functioning" institutional residents (a term used in the institution to identify those residents deemed skilled enough to go to school, undertake work, etc.), Margaret was forced to provide care for "low grade" or "low functioning" residents, including changing diapers and feeding. This labour was not only contrary to Margaret's desires, but also unremunerated. Margaret recalls a particular instance where she was forced to care for other residents when she did not want to. She recalls being tired and angry. Tears well up in her eyes as she remembers her frustration boiling over, causing her to punch a younger resident in her care. This memory is intensely painful; she recalls it with more emotive force and sorrow than she does memories of her own abuse. She is ashamed because the younger resident did not deserve to be punched, because this girl was just as much an institutional victim as she herself was.

Despite this, Margaret, like Connie, is an absolutely devoted pet owner. She owns two animals, a dog and a cat, and they share intensely cramped quarters in public housing – a crowded bachelor apartment no bigger than 200 square feet. Margaret struggles to make ends meet, but thinks nothing of spending several hours on the bus to ensure her dog Buster receives veterinary care, or has the food that he needs. Margaret has stories about Buster she recounts with warmth. When he is with her, bounding about workshop rooms or whinnying from her lap, she clutches him close to her, doting over him and seeking to calm and comfort him. In those moments, she tends to lean over to me (Jen), and to reiterate the earnest query: "Do you think I'm a good dog mama?" Like Connie and Midnight, it is clear that the relationship between Margaret and her animals is healing and reciprocal; Margaret's animals care for her as she cares for them. These animals mark a creative and resistant response to assuage loneliness, a way to give and receive love, to reimagine caregiving outside the boundaries of institutional harm.

One of the cruel ironies of institutionalization is the shifting dynamics of isolation and loneliness that have played out over survivors' lives. While incarcerated, residents lived in a kind of double state in regard to isolation: never alone, living in deeply overcrowded conditions bereft of privacy; but forcibly separated from friends, family, and a wider, non-resident

Embedded trauma, embodied resistance   89

community. Social and geographical isolation were central to the design and maintenance of institutions like Huronia and, we argue, this isolation played a crucial role in terms of the violence that occurred in such spaces.

One might presume that this isolation, and the concomitant loneliness that isolation creates, might end with deinstitutionalization, but in fact, survivors' lives often became reorganized around new forms of solitude and alienation long after leaving the physical confines of the institution. Once removed from the institution, residents scattered across Ontario. Indeed, our survivor-colleagues travelled from across the province to take part in our regular workshops. Thus, resident communities – communities of people who grew up in very close physical proximity and who bore witness to the same kinds of atrocities – were shattered. Many survivors, while able to live independently, had little access to the means to stay in touch with one another, while at the same time also had limited resources in terms of successfully integrating into 'mainstream' society. Survivors left the institution robbed of the skills, connections, and sense of community that would have enabled much fuller lives. This social marginalization was, of course, further compounded by ongoing financial precarity for many. Perhaps just as importantly, survivors also came away bearing the trauma and stigma attached to a diagnosis of intellectual disability and the experience of institutionalization, and few means to address or remediate these wrongs.

The impact of this isolation, particularly isolation from other survivors, became very clear through the settlement of the class action lawsuit brought by survivors of the Huronia Regional Centre. One of the unexpected outcomes of these proceedings was that it gave some survivors the chance to find one another after years of separation. Through the hard work of the litigation guardians, Huronia survivors from around the province convened at the courthouse to witness the proceedings, and then again at Queen's Park (the site of the Ontario provincial government) where Ontario Premier Kathleen Wynne delivered a public apology to those who had lived (and died) at Huronia. Survivors who had not seen one another for decades were overcome with the intensity of encountering long lost ward-mates. Often these survivors wept, holding one another, caressing one another's faces, assessing the impact of time, reimagining themselves as younger people, bound by the shared weight of institutional maltreatment. Of course, this makes perfect sense: who better might assuage an existential sense of isolation than those who share the same memories, who speak the *lingua franca* of collective violence and cruelty? For this reason, while recounting traumatic history and conducting political work can be taxing, survivors involved in the lawsuit and/or our research project have nevertheless found great comfort in forging connections and building community with one another, in sharing photographs and memories and candy, and expressing care.

Dress and song: social disgust and processing shame

Upon receiving his class action settlement cheque from the government, the first thing Ralph does is buy himself a brand new suit and leather jacket. The purchases complement a wardrobe that already garner him attention, for he is known for entering our workshop space in his sweeping trench coat, his polished suit and tie, even his double barrel black cowboy hat. He is a small man, a senior citizen with few teeth and a face wrinkled like an apple doll. An avid public speaker and Toastmaster member, he carries a professional briefcase filled with his public speaking trophies. Somehow, incredibly, he retains a defiant and absolute sense of optimism against a backdrop of despair. He remembers the day he left Huronia – and left behind his history of foster care – as liberatory, and he wears the mantle of survivor with pride.

Claire, too, has a complicated relationship with shame and pride borne out in her bodily presentation. Her childhood memories of her home and the institution, told and retold on loop, are punctuated with intense scenes of sexual violence. She states directly whenever sharing her history that she is telling the truth, that she did not want or invite the violence she experienced, that she was unhappy, as though she is warding off potential blame. She often tells these stories in her favourite purple, collared, button-down shirt and plum necktie – formal attire she is rather pleased to don, and to mark her as a butch lesbian. Sometimes she carries a wallet-sized professional photograph of herself in the purple clothing, a rainbow flag filling its background. That flag, emblematic of her reclaimed sexuality, she has had draped over her shoulders in workshop performances. That flag she has tattooed to her forearm, and she was thrilled to show it off the day I (Jen) met her. In these ways, Claire wears her pride.

For many of us who have not been the object of social disgust, it is easy to overlook or minimize the impact of shame in the lives of institutional survivors, and easy to ignore the long-term impacts of dehumanization arising from both institutional practices and the social beliefs that such practices operationalized. People with disabilities, intellectual disabilities in particular, have historically been, and in many cases remain, the object of social mistrust, hatred, and ridicule. The weight of social disgust is carried further by the experience of institutionalization, which not only inflicted long-lasting trauma and pain on survivors, but indelibly marked them as different, as social outcasts, as "spoiled" by stigma. This is to say that the very act of being institutionalized is a shameful marker of difference and marginalization, regardless of what happened during incarceration, and this difference has been profoundly internalized. Pam reminds us of this often, despairingly telling us that we "have no idea what it's like to be mentally retarded." Similarly, Margaret disparagingly refers to "people like us," meaning people who are developmentally disabled.

Embedded trauma, embodied resistance 91

Huronia, like other institutions, had no interest in aiding residents to look or feel valued or worthwhile. Rather, every institutional practice was designed to instil a sense of worthlessness in residents. These include mundane daily activities such as clothing oneself. David, for example, describes how routines around ordinary daily activities such as getting dressed imparted the institution's deep sense of disdain for residents' sense of social value, comfort and dignity:

> Fridays, you got a, uh a fresh change of clothes. Socks and underwear and pants and t-shirt. And that so the whole week, you've got the same clothes. And the same underwear everything so... During the week, uh you knew usually you washed out your own stuff. You'd put it on the radiator to dry so it would be dry in the morning. 'Cause you didn't get anything fresh until Friday. But uh and when the clothes like the socks, there would be a big sheet with all the clothes in it and tied up in a knot you've got this round bundle of clothes. So, there'd be pants in one and socks in one, underwear in one, and all kinds and so on and so on, and they'd untie that [bundle] to be all over the floor and you'd go and pick out yours, try to match a pair of socks and try to get a pair of pants to fit you. Everything was random, at random. Maybe the next pair of pants you get may be three sizes too big for ya sort of thing. Or a shirt that doesn't fit. And you'd be stuck with it for a week.

It is, then, a compellingly resistant strategy for Ralph and Claire to clothe themselves in the professional attire of a particular kind of masculinity, or masculine authority: the power suit. Robbed throughout childhood of the ability to choose their own forms of sartorial expression, they perform "businessman realness" by dressing in the costume of powerful men, thus propelling them into a different kind of life.

David's fight against the weight of institutional shame is markedly different, but no less brave. David was admitted to Huronia at the age of 11 following an illness that left him with "St. Vitus's Dance" (now called Sydenham's chorea) – a neurological disorder that causes tremors and other involuntary movements. David was re-tested and his diagnosis of developmental delay was withdrawn after his release from Huronia several years later. Staff had an inkling that he had been misdiagnosed, for he remembers a teacher at Huronia telling his parents that he did not belong there. This, however, did not persuade his parents to remove him from the institution. Instead, David ran away from the institution and was immediately returned to Huronia by his parents, whereupon he was badly beaten by staff as punishment for escaping.

While David can talk about his institutionalized life now, for most of his life he kept his past a secret. In fact, David, left the institution in his early adult years and went on to have a successful career, a wife and three daughters, none of whom knew that he had spent many years in Huronia. This

92 *Embedded trauma, embodied resistance*

changed for David when the class action lawsuit became public. It was at this point that David "came out" to his family and began speaking more openly about his time incarcerated. He explains that hearing a documentary about life at Huronia was a key turning point for him in revealing his past to his wife and children. "It was you", David tells Huronia lead plaintiff Patricia Seth over breakfast at the Orillia hotel at which we are all staying. "I heard you on the radio". He is referring to Pat's on-air description of the abuse she endured at Huronia, and her subsequent work as one of the two lead plaintiffs of the class action lawsuit. We are in Orillia for the site visit on the last day Huronia will be open to the public. David tells us that he hid his history for many years, but that something changed in him when he heard Pat speaking about her experience.

David has come to the site visit with his wife and youngest daughter, Jessie, a talented musician. Having just learned of David's incarceration, they are eager to see the place where he grew up. Together, the three of them move through the wards and hallways that once confined David and so many others. He shows his family where he slept, where he showered, where he escaped, and where he was beaten. His family is at once horrified and reverent – all three cry as they visit the spaces that have haunted him into later adulthood. Then, without prompting, Jessie pulls out her ukulele and begins to sing. The grain of her voice is beautiful and sad and melodic, echoing through empty hallways. As she sings, she begins to walk with her father through the building. Slowly, they move in and out of rooms, and her voice fills the echoing, cavernous corridors. She sings into pitch-dark side rooms where children were locked – traces of their tiny, desperate fingernails etched into the wooden doors. She sings into wards where residents endured countless nights of sexual abuse and torment. She sings into empty shower rooms where residents lost their dignity. She sings to the hallway, where her father was forced to stand holding a broom on outstretched hands for countless hours, countering the nightmare of captivity with the strength and grace of her voice. As they move together filling the space with music, David and his daughter prove that sometimes resistance and resilience is profoundly unpredictable, crossing generations, countering darkness with beauty, rupturing old patterns in unexpected ways.

Conclusions

These observations reveal that violence leaves a mark; that is, the biopolitical arrangements that produce and cultivate violence leave lasting impressions on the body. In this way, legacies of institutional violence haunt survivors, and carry long past their time spent institutionalized. Those legacies can be found in the habits, patterns, and practices performed in the home and community that reflect an extension or acknowledgment of institutional order. But where we find the residue of violence, we also find strategies for resistance – lived and enacted and embodied. Pam's haircut and Ralph's suit, the demand for pepperoni pizza toppings and the doting over a black cat, signal moments of subversion. Filling the hallways of the Huronia Regional Centre with wails and song transform the conditions of the space, or reconfigure the way power operates in that space. In these strategies are lessons in resilience, even when situational conditions are designed to grind the body down, in the ways violence does and does not define a person, in how to organize in the face and shadow of violence.

7 Conclusion

Throughout this book, we have argued that the very *design* of institutional care necessarily breeds a culture in which deep levels of violence are not only permissible, but normalized, and even encouraged. In the face of such an analysis, it is easy to feel hopeless about the potential for care without violence. Thus, we ask: what organizational models of care might facilitate adequate support while at the same time escaping violence? To end, we examine three different examples of social spaces designed to care for people with disabilities that are the organizational inverse of institutions and, as such, have minimized the possibilities for violence. Interestingly, these social spaces share particular commonalities. These include a commitment to communitarianism and life-sharing, a sense of higher purpose attached to caregiving efforts (particularly driven by spiritual or religious beliefs), a belief that care is mutual, and the understanding that all members of the community have the innate ability and desire to not only participate in community life, but to expand and enhance it. We contrast these models against the organizational attributes detailed in Chapter Two as a means of further iterating how these factors are implicated in fostering violence.

Camphill communities

Founded in the 1940s by Dr. Karl König (an Austrian Jewish paediatrician who fled to Britain in the 1930s to escape Nazism), the Camphill movement now boasts over 100 communities worldwide. Camphill communities are based on a model of life-sharing, and thus are spaces of intentional communal living designed to respectfully incorporate people with developmental disabilities into the daily life of the community. Communities are made up of several households, each of which is populated by "co-workers" (people who are not disabled) and "residents" or "companions" (people who live with developmental disability). Household members function as family units; indeed, many households contain whole families of co-workers who live in the community for decades, working, raising children and caring for companions. According to Luxford and Luxford (2003), Camphill communities are based on three pillars of social organization, each of which receive

Conclusion 95

attention and care. These are: "creating culture," through festivals, celebrations and community events; "rights, agreements, consultation and leadership," which has to do with meaningfully and intentionally sharing power and decision-making horizontally across the community; and "economic life," which has to do with creating generative and sustaining sites of work, such as in-house farms, bakeries, and potteries.

Based on the spiritual teachings of philosopher and educator Rudolf Steiner, König's Camphill movement goals were to "to create inclusive communities, where each person, according to their individual ability, contributes to the well-being of the whole" (Hart & Monteux, 2004, p. 67). Further, Steiner's belief in a "holistic understanding of each human being as a unique and essentially spiritual individual" translates into a series of community practices that uphold the abilities of *everyone* – companions and co-workers alike – and which help each community member to grow to their fullest social, spiritual, intellectual, and practical potential. The aim of these practices is to help co-workers "meet the unimpaired spiritual essence of companions" (Camphill School Aberdeen, 2015).

Hart and Monteux, who work at a Camphill community in Scotland, write that personal growth and development for all community members is supported by the vibrant educational and cultural life fostered by the movement:

> Depending on the particular population of the community, activities will have an emphasis on education or work; but all communities have in common a rich social, cultural and spiritual life. Daily living involves creative activities, active involvement in drama and musical events and the celebration of Christian and other festivals.
>
> (Hart & Monteux, 2004, p. 68)

This means that the whole community frequently comes together in joyous and meaningful ways that allow each community member to contribute their own unique gifts to the whole. Central to this is the notion that companions are just as responsible for participation and care for the community as co-workers. Care in this setting is not envisioned as a one-way street.

Beyond fostering an active and communitarian cultural life, Camphill communities strive to offer meaningful work, including gardening and farm work, craftwork and handwork, and cooking and baking for the community. These activities are meant less as an instrumental method of filling time, and more to support the development of inner qualities for each individual. While this may, on the surface, appear similar to the kind of work experiences offered in institutions and sheltered workshops, there is an enormous qualitative difference to the quality of the work and how it is accomplished. As a rule, Camphill community homes are designed to be beautiful, harmonious spaces. They are filled with light and work to incorporate elements of the natural world. Beauty, here, is a sign of deep respect

96 *Conclusion*

and support for the spiritual and aesthetic needs of the community members. Houses are kept clean not just for instrumental (i.e., health) purposes, but also because the houses are *homes* and treated with the kind of diligence one might treat a sacred space; co-workers are taught to clean with reverence and with the understanding that cleaning contributes to the life force and well-being of the whole community. Similar kinds of "dirty" caregiving jobs are understood as honourable because they support a larger spiritual and humanitarian goal. Thus, Camphill communities offer a holistic model of care that incorporates not only the well-being of each individual, but of the community itself.

L'Arche communities

Perhaps better known than the Camphill movement is the L'Arche movement, started by Canadian theologian Jean Vanier. Rooted in Roman Catholicism, Vanier began the L'Arche movement in the 1960s not only because of his horror regarding the marginalization and general maltreatment of institutionalized people with intellectual disabilities at the time, but also because of his belief that a communitarian lifestyle united by a larger sense of purpose was essential for the well-being of non-intellectually disabled people: "People cannot live as if they were on a desert island. They need companions, friends with whom they can share their lives, their visions and their ideas" (cited in Dunne, 1986, p. 41).

Vanier also believed that "retarded" people, who are often reliant on structures of community support, serve as a kind of existential challenge to the individualistic social ethos pervasive in the late twentieth century. Dunne writes:

> The acknowledgement of interdependence depends largely on qualities of the heart and necessitates a willingness to live close to one's own vulnerabilities and limitations, as well as those of one's neighbor. Thus, central to the l'Arche effort to [bear] witness to the possibility of creating a new society built on trust and interdependence is a very particular statement: that the weakest of our society the marginal deviant [sic], far from being a threat or an encumbrance, could be a teacher of the heart and a source of new hope.[1]
>
> (Dunne, 1986, p. 43)

From these sentiments, Vanier proposed a communitarian response to support people with intellectual disabilities and people without intellectual disabilities alike. The l'Arche movement had humble beginnings: Vanier invited two men with intellectual disabilities to come and live with him, to share his home and life. Like Camphill, the l'Arche movement now spans many countries, and comprises small, intentional communities designed to support people with intellectual disabilities in family-like settings. On their website, L'Arche Canada notes that "L'Arche seeks to provide environments where people can reach their full potential, lead lives rich in relationships of mutuality, and have a valid place in society where they can contribute" (2017, para. 4).

To do so, l'Arche communities are made up of several homes, which each house three to four "core members" (people with intellectual disabilities) and three to four "assistants" (people who do not live with intellectual disability). Unlike Camphill communities, which are often located in rural areas to support farming and gardening practices, many l'Arche communities are in urban areas where homes occupy the same neighborhood, and often share a communal space for celebrations, prayers, workshops and meetings (L'Arche Canada, 2017). Some l'Arche communities have day programs to support the learning and work of core members who cannot work in mainstream society. Like Camphill, l'Arche communities are built around a vision of social solidarity, mutual respect and the belief that the community supports the growth and development of *everyone's* best self. Caring, in this environment, is understood as a two-way street, and members of l'Arche communities believe the core members have a great deal to offer assistants (and others) in terms of care, support, and teaching.

Geel: City of Fools

Unique compared to the presented alternative models of care, Geel or the so-called City of Fools is located in Belgium. Geel has been a model for deinstitutionalized community care for people with psychiatric disabilities since the 1400s. The location is sacred for its association with Saint Dimpna, martyr and patron saint of 'the mentally ill.' According to lore, Dimpna was a seventh-century Irish princess who was chased to Geel by her father, who, upon finding her, beheaded his daughter. According to researchers Goldstein and Godemont (2003), during the Middle Ages, Geel became a pilgrimage site for "possessed pilgrims" – those with psychosis, obsessive compulsive disorder, intellectual disability, and other psychiatric conditions who had come to Geel in search of a remedy or cure, which took the form of "nine days of religious treatment" (p. 444). In deference to Dimpna, families in Geel began to take in pilgrims for whom nine days of treatment was not enough, housing and caring for them as if they were family. This developed into a system of in-home foster care, whereby foster families in Geel took on boarders with mental conditionso, often for periods of many years, and even decades.

Geel has persevered as a model of integrated community care and support for centuries, even in the face of the forceful institutionalization movement of the twentieth century, which forcefully sought to segregate and contain people with significant or severe psychiatric diagnoses. Naturally, however, the system of care has changed over time to reflect shifting views regarding the treatment of mental conditions, particularly as these treatments interface with the rise of modern psychiatry and the integration of health care with state practices. At times, these changes, alongside demographic and

98   *Conclusion*

cultural shifts, seemed to threaten Geel's tradition of family foster care – as the population of boarders waned from an all-time high of 3,800 in 1938, researchers in the 1970s and 1980s believed that Geel would not survive as a unique centre of psychiatric care (Godemont, 1992). However, traditional practices have persisted. A hospital serves as a site of primary diagnosis, assessment, and treatment; and provides a fallback, secondary support system and temporary rehabilitation centre should a boarder's condition become more than their foster family can manage. Further, each family is assigned a psychiatric nurse (see Goldstein & Godemont, 2003) who visits the family regularly and is on hand should a family experience difficulty.

In Geel, people with psychiatric disabilities do not just live with foster families; they are integrated into the whole community. Boarders work and live in Geel much like any other citizens. However, because of the centuries-old practices of embracing people with psychiatric disabilities, Geel is well positioned as a community to engage with and respond to people who live with difference. Goldstein and Godemont (2003) note that "because of their exposure to and experience with mental illness, the entire population protects rather than fears members of their community who are mentally ill" (p. 456). This seamless integration and sense of radical acceptance seems to have a profound effect on rates of violence. Unlike within institutional psychiatric settings, where violence among residents is often the norm, Geel is a remarkably peaceful place – indeed, part of Geel's overt collective "mission" is to subvert violence within the community, a goal which has been largely successful. Researcher Goosens (cited in Goldstein & Godemont, 2003) studied the rates of "delinquent occurrences" by boarders over a ten-year period in the 1970s and noted it was remarkably low. Goldstein similarly studied violence in Geel from 1996 to 2000 and confirmed this finding, anecdotally noting that from 1996 to the end of the 2002 calendar year, no incidences of violence had been reported in Geel (Goldestein & Godemont 2003, p. 452).

Organizational traits, revisited

Camphill, l'Arche, and Geel offer radically different approaches to the care and support of people with disabilities. These communities seem to have unchained themselves from the shackles of inhumanity and violence that have plagued institutional care settings. Importantly, these three models offer a direct organizational, and thus practical, rebuttal to the models offered within institutional settings, described in detail in Chapter Two, and revisited here in the light of alternate models of care.

Reform to radical acceptance

If the overarching goal of institutions is, in some respects, to reform or refashion its residents, Camphill, l'Arche, and Geel offer a powerful rebuke

Conclusion 99

to this aspect of institutional care through a conscious stance of *radical acceptance* of disability and, ultimately, human vulnerability and interdependence. This is to say that these communities do not think about intellectual or psychiatric disabilities, and their inevitable behavioural manifestations, as flaws that need to be corrected. They do not feel the need to 'normalize' or erase difference by way of conformity and uniformity. Rather, they acknowledge the deep individuality and vulnerability of *all* community members and find creative ways to support difference while upholding the belief that everyone can contribute meaningfully to the community.

Further, these communities understand that there is a great deal to be learned and gained by people without disabilities from people with disabilities. Goldstein, for example, relates a telling encounter with a foster mother in Geel that took place during her research. The foster mother cared for a boarder whose obsessions led him to pull the buttons off his garments every day. And every day, the foster mother sewed the buttons back onto the garments. When Goldstein asked why she did not, for example, affix the buttons back on with fishing line or some other less breakable material, the foster mother appeared horrified. She said: "no, no you don't understand – that's the worst thing you could do ... I will never use fishing line because this man *needs* to twist the buttons off. It helps him to twist them off every day" (cited in Spiegel & Rosin, 2016). Gaston VanDyke, a fellow Geel resident and friend of Goldstein's elaborates: "The philosophy behind that is first you have to accept mentally ill people. You have to accept what they are doing" (Spiegel & Rosin 2016). Similarly, another host mother casually recounted the ways in which she dealt with a boarder experiencing hallucinations of lions coming through the walls, explaining that she simply (and effectively) just chased the lions away.

In fact, Geel's model of care runs so contrary to the modern psychiatric movement, that foster families are not told of their guests' diagnoses – these diagnoses, foster families feel, are restrictive to everyone and do not allow boarders to live in the family and community in unfettered ways. Goldstein argues that this kind of radical acceptance, and not the impulse to cure, fix or remediate, is deeply healing, and has allowed many who have been plagued by their afflictions in other settings to live happily and peaceably in Geel. This is, of course, not just a gift to the boarders, but to the whole community, which is enriched by their presence. Jean Vanier summarizes the importance of such acceptance, writing:

In our mad world where there is so much pain, rivalry, hatred, violence, inequality, and oppression, it is people who are weak, rejected, marginalized, counted as useless, who can become a source of life and of salvation for us as individuals as well as for our world.

(cited in Dunne, 1986, p. 43)

100   Conclusion

Austerity to generosity

Alongside an acceptance, and even embrace, of difference, Camphill, l'Arche, and Geel also differ from institutional settings in terms of cultivating an ethos of *generosity* and *abundance* rather than austerity and deprivation. Here, again, we envision generosity and abundance broadly, meaning that while these communities may not necessarily boast a sense of economic wealth per se, there is an overall sense of social, cultural, and spiritual generosity. These are particularly articulated in Camphill and l'Arche, where the actions of giving and sharing form the basis of many of the cultural practices that occur. Potlucks, communal dinner, and shared celebration cement these communities, and mean that everyone is part of a cultural economy that involves making sure that care – by way of food and pleasure – is abundant and enjoyed by all.

A former co-worker at an Ontario Camphill community, for example, recounts this attitude of generosity expressed particularly through the provision of food. This co-worker lived alongside a companion who had been previously institutionalized. This companion was afflicted by the need to eat compulsively, despite its harm to her overall health. While afflictions like these were treated punitively within institutional settings, co-workers at Camphill addressed the situation with creativity and care. First, while the kitchen remained off limits to this companion (as she was unable to stop herself from eating its contents), at dinner she was served her very own "bottomless" salad. This salad, made just for her, was hearty and decorated beautifully with a variety of vegetables and radish rosettes and came to the table looking like a work of art. Rather than depriving her of food, she was instead allowed to eat as much of the beautiful salad as she liked. Second, the community gave her a cat, which was hers to feed and care for. Here, the idea was that instead of feeding herself, some of her energy and attention would be placed onto the cat, for whom she was responsible. This proved very important as the cat become deeply beloved by this companion, who constantly reminded the cat that she would never leave for long and would come back to feed it soon. While such an affliction could have been managed through increasingly heavy-handed rules, restrictions, and punishments, this community chose to respond with a sense of creative abundance which allowed the companion to flourish.

Isolation to life-sharing

While institutional practices hinge on the isolation of residents in multiple ways – socially, geographically, emotionally – Camphill, l'Arche, and Geel rest on a completely different model: that of intensive life sharing. This means that people without disabilities not only live and work with people with disabilities, but are actively involved in sharing all kinds of life events as you would with any family member: meals, trips, parties, etc. This

Conclusion 101

differs radically from institutional practices, which by design foster a sense of deep isolation. Within institutions, workers come for shifts, then return to their home and community, ensuring that institutional residents understand that they are outside the bounds of who counts as a viable community member. In these three alternate instances, however, community is formed with and around people with disabilities: they are at the centre rather than the margins – they are the *reason* for community, not its antithesis. Dunne (1986), for example, writes "in l'Arche, community is not just for or with, but essentially *through* the retarded [sic] member" (p. 43).

In practice, this of course looks very different from an institutional model. Those who live with disability occupy homes with those who do not. Gone is the architecture that underlines and reinforces difference: austere buildings set away from other living spaces, where residents are crammed onto wards, forced to eat in large cafeterias, all managed through constant staff surveillance. Rather, these are 'normal' homes featuring kitchens and living spaces accessible to all. Meals are eaten communally; everyone recreates together. Further, many of the L'Arche communities are located at the heart of urban centres rather than away from them. These communities are open and porous to with the wider community, where some residents may work and play. Geel, of course, takes this one step further, fully integrating people with mental illness into the community, so much so that the very identity of the community is tied to the embrace and acceptance of difference and disability. Here, again, there is no firm "us" and "them". Indeed, a local aphorism jokes that "half of Geel is crazy and the rest are half crazy," suggesting a loose and comfortable boundary between those diagnosed with psychiatric disability and the 'normal' population.

Social denigration to shared humanity

Finally, but perhaps most importantly, these three examples of alternate care organize themselves not around an instrumental need (i.e., the management and containment of people with disabilities) but around a *shared humanitarian vision* exemplified and articulated through the work of caregiving and community building. In other words, caregiving, life sharing, and community building suggest something about a larger aspirational vision regarding humanity and the world. For all three models of care, this aspirational vision necessarily includes the deep acknowledgement of people with disabilities as whole, as individual, as capable, and as distinctly *human*. Given how these models of care are organized, this may be obvious, as to meaningfully share one's life with another person, you must encounter them as a fellow human being, which is to say, a whole person. This belief, of course, is operationalized through a system of care that works to greet and support the humanity of each of its community members, by acknowledging and responding to needs, finding forms of work and play that support the community, collectively marking life's joys and sorrows, and sharing space,

102　*Conclusion*

resources, time, and care. This is perhaps exemplified by the (non-disabled) community member from Geel who, when asked if the care for people with disabilities was a burden, seemed stymied by the question, and quizzically answered: "it's just normal life – I don't see it as being painful" (Spiegel & Rosin, 2016).

It is perhaps this shared vision of humanity, and insistent belief in the personhood of people with disabilities, that allows these communities to function without the level of violence so often found in other care settings. Bandura (1999) reminds us that dehumanization is the surest route to violence but, conversely, that the work of humanizing a group of people causes the *cessation* of violence. He writes that "social practices that divide people into in-group and outgroup members produce human estrangement that fosters dehumanization" but, crucially, that:

> the power of humanization to counteract cruel conduct also has considerable social import. People's recognition of the social linkage of their lives and their vested interest in each other's welfare help to support actions that instil them with a sense of community. The affirmation of common humanity can bring out the best in others.
>
> (Bandura, 1999, p. 203)

This, of course, is what we see in action in Camphill communities, l'Arche communities, and in Geel.

We end on such a hopeful tone because we believe we owe it to institutional survivors to do better imagining and constructing the conditions of care. We can across regions, and time, and institutional models chart the inevitability of violence against those institutionalized. Through this book we endeavoured to demonstrate how institutional violence becomes possible and permissible, and in so doing we have sought to establish that because of the violence it espouses institutionalization is unjust. May the world cultivate more Camphills and l'Arches and Geels, because persons with disabilities should never have to ensure another Huronia.

Note

1 This view has been refuted as patronizing by some members of the disability community. See, for example, Lee, 1991.

Bibliography

Abbas, J., & Voronka, J. (2014) Remembering institutional Erasures: The meaning of histories of disability incarceration in Ontario. In L. Ben-Moshe, C. Chapman, A.C. Carey (eds.), *Disability Incarcerated: Imprisonment and Disability in the United States and Canada* (pp. 121–138) New York, NY: Palgrave Macmillan.

Alamenciak, T. (2014) Remembering the dead at Huronia Regional Centre. *The Toronto Star,* December 29. Retrieved from http://www.thestar.com

Arendt, H. (1963) *Eichmann in Jerusalem: A Report on the Banality of Evil.* New York, NY: The Viking Press.

Arendt, H. (1970) *On Violence.* New York, NY: Harcourt.

Arendt, H. (1978) *The Life of the Mind: The Groundbreaking Investigation on How We Think.* New York, NY: Harcourt.

Arendt, H. (1982) *Lectures on Kant's Political Philosophy.* Chicago, IL: University of Chicago Press.

Arendt, H., & Jaspers, K. (1946) Letter 46. In *Correspondence, 1926–1969.* New York, NY: Harcourt.

Armstrong, F. (2002) The historical development of special education: humanitarian rationality or 'wild profusion of entangled events'? *History of Education, 31*(5), 437–456.

BakerLaw (2014) Common principles on the inclusion of people with disabilities in their communities. *Institutionalization as a Form of Discrimination*, Sepember 24. Retrieved from http://www.bakerlaw.ca

Bandura, A. (1999) Moral disengagement in the perpetration of inhumanities. *Personality and Social Psychology Review, 3,* 193–209.

Bandura, A. (2002) Social cognitive theory in cultural context. *Applied Psychology: An International Review, 51*(2), 269–290.

Bandura, A. (2006) Toward a psychology of human agency. *Perspectives on Psychological Science, 1*(2), 164–180.

Bandura, A., Barbaranelli, C., Caprara, G.V., & Pastorelli, C. (1996) Multifaceted impact of self-efficacy beliefs on academic functioning. *Child Development, 67,* 1206–1222.

Barker v Barker (2017) OJ No. 2808.

Barthes, R. (1977) *Image-Music-Text.* New York, NY: Hill & Wang.

Baynton, D. (1998) *Forbidden Signs: American Culture and the Campaign Against Sign Language.* Chicago: University of Chicago Press.

Bechard v Ontario Statement of Claim (2010) Court File No. CV-10–417343-00CP.

104 Bibliography

Bell, R. (2013, June 30) New book explores lives of patients at HRC. *Orillia Packet & Times*. Retrieved from: http://www.orilliapacket.com

Ben-Moshe, L. (2014) Alternatives to (disability) incarceration. In L. Ben-Moshe, C. Chapman, & A. Carey (eds.), *Disability Incarcerated: Imprisonment and Disability in the United States and Canada* (pp. 255–272). New York, NY: Palgrave Macmillan.

Berton, P. (1960) What's wrong at Orillia: Out of sight, out of mind. *Toronto Daily Star*, January 6. Retrieved from https://www.thestar.com/news/insight/2013/09/20/huronia_pierre_berton_warned_us_50_years_ago.html

Broderick, R. (2011) *Empty hallways, unheard voices: The deinstitutionalization narratives of staff and residents at the Huronia*. (Unpublished major research paper). Toronto, ON: York University.

Burghardt, M. (2016) "It was the worst place I ever lived"; "It was the best place I ever worked": Narrative discrepancy as a nexus of oppression, Canadian Disability Studies Association Annual Conference, University of Calgary, May 28–30.

Butler, J. (1990) *Gender Trouble: Feminism and the Subversion of Identity*. New York, NY: Routledge.

Camphill School Aberdeen (2015) *Camphill Co-worker Information Handbook*. Retrieved from http://www.camphillschools.org.uk

Caplan, E. (1991) *Multi–year Plan for Deinstitutionalization of Developmentally Handicapped People in Ontario*. Toronto, ON: Ontario Legislative Assembly Standing Committee on Social Development.

Castellano, M.B., Archibald, L. & DeGagné, M. (eds.) (2008) *From Truth to Reconciliation: Transforming the Legacy of Residential Schools*. Ottawa, ON: Aboriginal Healing Foundation.

CBC News. (2014) Michener Centre closure halted, residents allowed to return, September 19. Retrieved from http://www.cbc.ca/news

CBC News (2013) Huronia Regional Centre lawsuit ends in $35M settlement: Residents of defunct centre operated by province alleged abuse happened daily, September 13 Retrieved from www.cbc.ca/news.

Centre de la communauté sourde du Montréal métropolitain c. Clercs de Saint-Viateur du Canada (2016) JQ No. 5742.

Chapman, C. (2010) Becoming perpetrator: How I came to accept restraining and confining disabled aboriginal children, PsychOut: A Conference for Organizing Resistance Against Psychiatry, OISE, Toronto, May 7–9.

Charges MPP pressure jam mental hospital. (1960) *Toronto Daily Star*, January 8.

Chima, F. (1998) Familial, institutional, and societal sources of elder abuse: perspective on empowerment. *International Review of Modern Sociology, 28*(1), 103–116.

Chupik, J., & Wright, D. (2006) Treating the 'idiot' child in early 20th-century Ontario. *Disability & Society, 21*(1), 77–90.

Cloud et al. v Canada (Attorney General) (2004) OJ No. 4924.

Cohen, E. (2009) *A Body Worth Defending: Immunity, Biopolitics, and the Apotheosis of the Modern Body*. Durham, NC: Duke University Press.

Dolmage v Ontario (2010) ONSC 1726.

Dolmage v Ontario (2010) ONSC 6131.

Dolmage v Ontario Statement of Defence (2011) Court File No. CV-09–376927-CP00.

Dolmage v Her Majesty the Queen (2013) ONSC 6686.

Dolmage, McKillop and Bechard v Her Majesty the Queen (2014) ONSC 1283.

Drinkwater, C. (2015) Supported living and the production of individuals. In S. Tremain (ed.), *Foucault and the Government of Disability* (pp. 229–244). Ann Arbor, MI: University of Michigan Press.

Bibliography   105

Dunne, J. (1986) Sense of community in L'Arche and the writings of Jean Vanier. *Journal of Community Psychology, 14*(1), 41–54.

Dyck, E. (2013) *Facing Eugenics: Reproduction, Sterilization, and the Politics of Choice.* Toronto, ON: University of Toronto Press.

Eggleston v Barker (2003) OJ No. 3137.

Elwin v Nova Scotia Home for Colored Children (2013) NSJ No. 668.

Felman, S. (2002) *The Juridical Unconscious: Trials and Traumas in the Twentieth Century.* Cambridge, MA: Harvard University Press.

Foucault, M. (1978) *The History of Sexuality. Volume 1: An Introduction* (R. Hurley, Trans.). New York, NY: Pantheon Books.

Foucault, M. (1979) *Discipline and Punish: The Birth of the Prison* (A. Sheridan, Trans.). New York, NY: Vintage Books.

Fraser, M., & Greco, M. (2005) *The Body: A Reader.* New York, NY: Routledge.

Gimlin, D. (2006) The absent body: cosmetic surgery as a response to bodily dysappearance. *Sociology, 40*(4), 699–716.

Godemont, M. (1992) 600 years of family care in Geel, Belgium: 600 years of familiarity with madness in town life. *Community Alternatives: International Journal of Family Care, 4*(2), 155–168.

Goffman, E. (1961) *Asylums: Essays on the Social Situation of Mental Patients and Other Inmates.* New York, NY: Penguin.

Goffman, E. (1963) *Stigma: Notes on the Management of Spoiled Identity.* London, UK: Penguin.

Goffman, E. (2007) *Asylums: Essays on the Social Situation of Mental Patients and Other Inmates.* Piscataway, NJ: Transaction Publishers.

Gold, E. (2016) By any other name: an exploration of the academic development of torture and its links to the military and psychiatry. In B. Burstow (ed.), *Psychiatry Interrogated: An Institutional Ethnography Anthology* (pp. 203–226). New York, NY: Springer.

Goldstein, J.L., & Godemont, M.M.L. (2003) The Legend and Lessons of Geel, Belgium: A 1500-Year-Old Legend, a 21st-Century Model. *Community Mental Health Journal, 39*(5), 441–458.

Gutnick, D. (2011) The gristle in the stew: revisiting the horrors of Huronia. *The Doc Project.* Toronto, ON: Canadian Broadcast Corporation. Retrieved from http:// www.cbc.ca

davis halifax, n., Fancy, D., Rinaldi, J., Rossiter, K., & Tigchelaar, A. (2017) Recounting Huronia faithfully: attenuating our methodology to the 'fabulation' of *truths*-telling. *Cultural Studies <———> Critical Methodologies, 12*(1), 1–12.

Hammersley, P., & Atkinson, M. (1995) *Ethnography: Principles in Practice* (2nd edn). New York, NY: Routledge.

Hart, N., & Monteux, A. (2004) An introduction to Camphill communities and the BA in Curative Education. *Scottish Journal of Residential Child Care, 3*(1), 67–74.

Heckert, C. (2016) When care is a 'systematic route of torture': conceptualizing the violence of medical negligence in resource-poor settings. *Culture, Medicine, and Psychiatry 40*(4), 687–706.

Hlady, M., & Migone, C. (2017) Soundfull: a wall speaks, a door shakes, a floor trembles. *Canadian Journal of Disability Studies, 6*(3), 215–228.

Inge, W.R. (1909) Some moral aspects of eugenics. *The Eugenics Review 1*(1), 26–36.

Johnson, K., & Traustadóttir, R. (eds.) (2005) *Deinstitutionalization and People with Intellectual Disabilities: In and Out of Institutions.* Vancouver, BC: Jessica Kingsley.

106 Bibliography

Koskie Minsky LLP. (2015) Huronia Regional Centre Claims Process Materials. Retrieved from http://www.kmlaw.ca

L'Arche Canada. (2017) Help us build a world where everyone belongs. Retrieved from www.larche.ca

Larson, L., & Haddad. S. (2016) A Message from the task force. *People First of Canada, 10*(1) Winnipeg, MB: Institution Watch 1.

Law Commission of Canada (2000) *Restoring Dignity – Responding to Child Abuse in Canadian Institutions: Executive Summary.* Ottawa, ON: Minister of Public Works and Government Services.

Lee, John. 1991. Jean Vanier & L'Arche: A communion of love. *Disability, Handicap & Society, 6*(1), pp. 73–74.

Luhmann, N. (1985) *A Sociological Theory of Law.* Boston, MA: Routledge.

Luhmann, N. (1989) Law as a social system. *Northwestern University Law Review 83*(1&2), 136–150.

Luxford, J., & Luxford, M. (2003) *A Sense for Community: the Camphill Movement: a Five Steps Research Paper 2003.* Botton Village, UK: Camphill Books.

Malacrida, C. (2012) Bodily practices as vehicles for dehumanization in an institution for 'Mental Defectives'. Special Issue "Embodied action, embodied theory: understanding the body in society". *Societies, 2,* 286–301.

Malacrida, C. (2015) *A Special Hell: Institutional Life in Alberta's Eugenic Years.* Toronto, ON: University of Toronto Press.

McKillop v Ontario Statement of Claim (2010) Court File No. CV-10–411191.

McIntyre v Ontario (2016) OJ No. 2205.

McIntyre v Ontario Statement of Claim (2014) Court File No. CV-14–506421-00CP.

Mechanic, D., & Rochefort, D.A. (1990) Deinstitutionalization: An appraisal of reform. *Annual Review of Sociology, 16,* 301–327.

Milgram, S. (1974) *Obedience to Authority: An Experimental View.* New York, NY: Harper-Collins.

Mitchell, D.T., & Snyder, S.L. (2015) *The Biopolitics of Disability: Neoliberalism, Ablenationalism, and Peripheral Embodiment.* Ann Arbor, MI: University of Michigan Press.

Mosby, I., & Galloway, T. (2017) 'The abiding condition was hunger': assessing the long–term biological and health effects of malnutrition and hunger in Canada's residential schools. *British Journal of Canadian Studies, 30*(2), 147–162.

Orillia Charges 'True'. (1960) *Toronto Daily Star,* January 7.

Park, D.C. (1990) *Changing shadows: The Huronia Regional Centre, 1876–1934.* (Doctoral dissertation) Retrieved from ProQuest Dissertations and Theses. (Accession No. 0315905050)

Park, D.C., & Radford, J.P. (1998) From the case files: reconstructing a history of involuntary sterilisation. *Disability & Society, 13*(3), 317–342.

Reaume, G. (1997) Accounts of abuse of patients at the Toronto Hospital for the Insane, 1883–1937. *Canadian Bulletin of Medical History, 14,* 65–106.

Rossiter, K., & Clarkson, A. (2013) Opening Ontario's "saddest chapter": a social history of Huronia Regional Centre. *Canadian Journal of Disability Studies, 2*(3), 1–28.

Roy, S. (2015) Former Rideau staff seek Premier's apology through online petition. *Smith Falls Record News,* January 22. Retrieved from https://www.insideotta wavalley.com

Rumley v British Columbia [2001] 3 SCR 184.

Bibliography 107

Sansome, S. (2014) Reader feels plaque is offensive. *Smith Falls Recorded News*, December 25. Retrieved from https://www.insideottawavalley.com.

Scarry, E. (1985) *The Body in Pain: The Making and Unmaking of the World*. New York, NY: Oxford University Press.

Sherr, L., Roberts, K.J., & Gandhi, N. (2017) Child violence experiences in institutionalised/orphanage care. *Psychological Health Medicine, 22*(suppl. 1), 31–57.

Seed v Ontario (2012) OJ No. 2006.

Seed v Ontario (2017) OJ No. 2958.

Sherr, L., Roberts, K.J., & Gandhi, N. (2017) Child violence experiences in institutionalised/orphanage care. *Psychological Health Medicine, 22*(suppl. 1), 31–57.

Shildrick, M. (1997) *Leaky Bodies and Boundaries: Feminism, Postmodernism and (Bio)ethics*. London, UK: Routledge.

Shilling, C. (1993) *The Body and Social Theory*. Thousand Oaks, CA: SAGE.

Shilling, C. (1997) Emotions, embodiment and the sensation of society. *The Sociological Review, 45*(2), 195–219.

Simmons, H.G. (1982) *From Asylum to Welfare*. Toronto, ON: National Institute on Mental Retardation.

Spiegel, E., & Rosin, A. (2016) The problem with the solution. *Invisibilia*, July 1. Retrieved from www.npr.org

Stenfert Kroese, B., & Holmes, G. (2013) "I've never said 'No' to anything in my life": Helping people with learning disabilities who experience psychological problems. In C. Newnes, G. Holmes, & C. Dunn (eds,), *This is Madness Too: Critical Perspectives on Mental Health Issues* (pp. 71–80). Monmouth, UK: PCCS Books.

Stewart, J., & Russell, M. (2001) Disablement, prison, and historical segregation. *Monthly Review: An Independent Socialist Magazine, 53*(3), 1–7.

Stuckey, Z. (2013) In pursuit of the common life: rhetoric and education at the New York State Asylum for "Idiots" at Syracuse, 1854–1884. *Rhetoric Review, 32*(3), 233–249.

Sullivan, P., McCay V., & Scanlan, J. (1987) Sexual abuse of deaf youth. *American Annals of the Deaf 132*(4), 256–262.

Surviving Huronia. (2014, December 2) Tangled Art + Disability. Retrieved from http://tangledarts.org

Templin v Her Majesty the Queen (2016) ONSC 7853.

Templin v Her Majesty the Queen Statement of Claim (2016) Court File No. CV-16–547155-00CP.

Tremain, S. (ed.) (2015) *Foucault and the Government of Disability*. Ann Arbor, MI: University of Michigan Press.

Turner, B. (1992) *Regulating Bodies: Essays in Medical Sociology*. New York, NY: Routledge.

Urban Walker, M. (2014) Moral vulnerability and the task of teparations. In C. Mackenzie, W. Rogers, & S. Dodds (eds.), *Vulnerability: New Essays in Ethics and Feminist Philosophy* (pp. 111–133). New York, NY: Oxford University Press.

Van Haute, P. (1998) Death and sublimation in Lacan's reading of *Antigone*. In S. Harasym (ed.), *Levinas and Lacan: The Missed Encounter* (pp. 102–120) Albany, NY: State University of New York Press.

Welch, R. (1973) *Community Living for the Mentally Retarded in Ontario: A New Policy Focus*. Ottawa, ON: Provincial Secretary for Social Development.

Welsh v Ontario (2016) ONSC 5319.

108 *Bibliography*

Welsh v Ontario Statement of Claim (2016) Court File No. CV-15-534042-00CP.

Wieviorka, M. (2010) *Violence: A New Approach.* London, UK: SAGE.

Williams, S. (1987) Goffman, interactionism, and the management of stigma in everyday life. In G. Scambler (ed.), *Sociological Theory and Medical Sociology* (pp. 134–164). London, UK: Tavistock.

Williston, W.B. (1971) *A report to The Honourable A.B.R. Lawrence, Minister of Health on present arrangements for the care and supervision of mentally retarded persons in Ontario.* Toronto, ON: Ontario Department of Health.

Wright, D. (2011) *Downs: The history of a disability.* Oxford, UK: Oxford University Press.

Wynne, K. (2013, December 9) *Ontario's Apology to Former Residents of Regional Centres for People with Developmental Disabilities.* Ontario Ministry of Community and Social Services. Retrieved from http://www.mcss.gov.on.ca

Zimbardo, P. (2007) *The Lucifer Effect: Understanding How Good People Turn Evil.* New York, NY: Random House.

Index

Abbas, J. 8
abundance 100
abuse: abusers 79, 84, 88; allegations of 19, 62; as caregiving routine 53; case law 27; in childhood 1, 73; conditions of possibility 34, 74; emotional 14, 69; history of 87, 88; institutional 23, 25–6, 61, 71, 77; levels of 70; physical 2, 14; prevention of 31; psychological 14, 69; as punishment 6, 29; role of the state in perpetuating 66; routine 52, 77, 92; in settlement 67, 69–70; sexual 26; by students 33; verbal 28; *see also* humiliation; punishment; violence
addiction 2
administration 26, 69–70, 81
administrators 9, 11, 20, 32, 34, 56
adolescents *see* youth
adulthood 15, 92
adults 7, 9, 15, 17, 35, 84
American Sign Language *see* language
anxiety 2, 81
apology *see* public apology
architecture 32, 101
archival data 13
Arendt, H. 20, 56–9, 62–6
arts-based ethnographic methodologies *see* ethnographic methodologies
assault *see* sexual assault; violence
asylums 3, 5–10, 40, 68, 73, 82
attitudes 6, 74
austerity 31, 85–6, 100; *see also* institutional model
autonomy 30, 37, 40, 85

'bad apple' behaviour 24, 27, 61, 72
banality of evil 20, 56, 58, 63–5; *see also* evil
Bandura, A.: dehumanization 35, 102; moral abdication 28–29, 32;

moral failing 24–6; situational moral disengagement 19, 23
Banduran theory 23, 28, 34, 36
Barker v Barker 28, 30, 34–6
Barthes, R. 79
bath 16, *17*, 48
bathing 6, 16, 19, 45–6
bathroom 1, 35, 44, 53, 71
beatings 1, 29, 47, 49, 52–3, 91–2
Bechard v Ontario 29, 31–2, 35
bed wetting 30, 44
behaviour 25, 29, 59, 71, 74, 99: damaging 25; demeaning 70; inhumane 25; institutional 56; misbehaviour 50; modification 25, 26, 30, 46–7, 51, 53; non-consensual (sexual) 70; self-regulatory 25, 34; violent 60; *see also* 'bad apple' behaviour
Berton, P. 10–13
Binnie, I. 70, 76 n2
biopower 81, 83; *see also* Foucault, M.
blindness 5–6, 13, 27, 33, 36
body: agency 35, 79; comportment 34; control 26, 36, 50, 55; corporeal care 49; degradation 1, 3, 5, 43, 50; routines 34, 37; surveillance 43–6; weight 44–5, 85; *see also* care; embodiment
buildings: antiquated 31; making sound on 79; re-visiting 16; as sites of danger and death 11–12; site visit to 92; as tools of seclusion 6; tunnels in 51; as warehouses for disabled 33; *see also* Huronia Regional Centre; sound
Butler, J. 82

cages *see* cribs
Camphill: communities 55, 94–8, 100, 102; movement 21
care: alternate models of 21, 94–102; caregiving 2–4, 87–8, 94, 96, 101;

110 Index

care-*qua*-violence 39; to deny bodily autonomy 37, 45; failures of 46, as forms of daily violence 2, 19; routines 34; settings 2, 4, 94; sexual abuse 53
case law *see* legal proceedings
cats *see* pets
cemetery 14, 18, 54–5, 69, 75; *see also* Huronia Regional Centre
Chapman, C. 59–60
children: in Camphill communities 94; in caged cots 17, 71; care and treatment for 9; 'defective' or disabled 5–6, 13, 68; methods of treating 5; necessity of institutional care 11; parent-child relationship 63; rationalizing restraint of 60; residents 92; of survivors 87, 92
Children's Aid Society 9
chronic deprivation *see* deprivation
chronic pain 1, 49
Chupik, J. 5, 7, 9
City of Fools *see* Geel (Belgium)
civil litigation *see* legal proceedings
class action lawsuit: allegations 5; analysis 26, 28; evidence 62; importance of HRC against government of Ontario 1, 8, 13, 67, 72; insights from 23; Institutional Cases 14, 19; language 20; outcomes 89, 92; parameters of 15; re-traumatization 20; Seth 78; settlement 27, 61, 90; *see also* Institutional Cases; legal proceedings
Clements, M. 61–2
clothing 30–2, 43, 46–7, 71, 90–1; *see also* dress
coercion 35, 57, 69
cognition: cognitive mechanisms 25–6, 28, 36; cognitive shifts 25–6, 29, 32, 36; social cognitive development 25
"cold" violence *see* violence
community: activism 55; building 76, 89; efforts to promote care 13, 75; lack of support 11–12; as model of care 8, 21, 33, 55, 94–101; practices performed in 92; productive members of 15; sense of 54, 89; separation from 74, 89
compensation 14, 21, 65–7, 69–70, 72–3, 75; *see also* settlement
compliance 29–30, 46–7, 53, 85
confinement 35: conditions of 48; indefinite 74; in late 19th century 6; necessity of 60; beyond physical 89; *see also* solitary confinement
conformity 46, 83, 85, 99

conscience 59–60
consent 28, 35; *see also* non-consensual behaviour
court, civil 73: attendance 80; day in 15, 65; juridical function of 65; preparation for 1, 15; record of cases 14; settlement 27; settlement out of 8, 13–14, 15, 67, 70; *see also* settlement
courtroom 27, 65–6, 72–3
cribs 16, 17, 71
criticality 20, 56, 66
critical theory 13, 15
cultural attitudes *see* attitudes
curative treatments 28

death 54, 74: camps (Holocaust) 58; at Orillia's Hospital School 11; at Huronia Regional Centre 18, 50, 54, 89; remembering the dead 54; of residents' family members 87; starvation 44; threat of 50
dehumanization: cognitive shifts 36; in concentration camps 65; control 35; disabled persons 34; human estrangement 102; incarcerated human as institutional object 29; influence on perception of subject 26; institutionalization 34, 40, 43, 54, 73; long-term impacts of 90; Malacrida 40, 41; marker of 33; routine 41; social position 34; surveillance 41; thoughtlessness 60; violence 34, 39, 40, 41, 55, 102; *see also* violence
deinstitutionalization 8, 13, 15, 65, 74, 89; *see also* institutionalization
depression 2, 15
deprivation 31, 74, 85–6, 100: chronic 85; sensory 33
diapers 71, 88
dignity: absence of in death 54; alternate models of care 21; challenges of ensuring within institutions 46; human 25, 41, 35, 46; negation of 30, 43, 46, 50, 91, 92; *see also* indignity
disability: abuse 74; acknowledgment of harm towards 74, 86; alternate models of care 21, 55, 94–102; court cases 14, 19, 26–7, 32–35, 69, 73; dehumanization 40; developmental 2, 8, 33, 68, 90, 94; historical perceptions of 2–4, 5–6, 8–11, 34, 68, 90; institutional violence 1–4, 13, 25–6, 28; intellectual 6, 7, 75; isolation 63; marginalization 2, 34; medicalization

74; physical 4, 17, 28; psychiatric 2, 8, 19, 28, 101; *Recounting Huronia* research group members 15; social discourse 82; stigma 74, 89; as threat 74; in total institutions 1–2, 4, 6, 13, 27, 71
disability justice 14
disability studies 13, 80, 82
discipline 29–30, 51, 54, 57, 65, 81–3
discourse 32, 56, 81–2: legal 14, 67; medical 6; social 82
discourse analysis 3, 20
disempower 67; *see also* power
disgust 31, 90
dogs *see* pets
Dolmage, J. and M. 12, 13, 37n4, 67
Dolmage, McKillop and Bechard v HMQ 27, 72
Dolmage v HMQ 27, 69–70
Dolmage v Ontario 2010: 14, 29, 31, 69–70, 75; Statement of Defence 2011 33, 35
dress 43, 50, 83, 90–1 *see also* clothing
dumbness 5
dyads *see* research dyads
Dymond, M.B. 12

eating 16, 19; and care 85; control over 41, 45, 85, 86, 100; and emotion 86–87; pleasure of 85; punishments for not 30; schedules 29; *see also* feeding; food; meals
Edgar, Adult Occupational Centre in the town of 27, 29
education: alternate models of care 95; challenge to maintain after institutionalization 2, 86; and control 29, 41; educational leaflet 68; educational system 9; efforts to educate disabled peoples 5–6, 7, 33; health 35; historical beliefs about 6; substandard 36, 71; treatment-based 6
efficiency *see also* institutional model
Eggleston v Barker 35
Eichmann, A. 58–60, 64–5
elderly 2, 9
electric shock 29
embodiment: Butler 82; ethos of austerity 86; experiences of 79; Foucault 81; identity 80; individuality 85; management strategies 81; reproduction of institutionalization 79; resistance 93; of social memory 76; *see also* resistance

empathy 59, 62, 66
escape 52, 91–2, 94
ethnographic methodologies 16: arts-based 16, 18–19; data 8, 39; observation 3, 13, 18, 39, 79; workshops 18, 39, 80, 86–90, 95, 97
eugenics 7, 68
evil 66, 87: Arendt 59, 64–5; Bandura 26; legal instruments to approach 20, 57; as problem of morality 26; situational 41; Zimbardo 24, 41; *see also banality of evil*
extreme violence: between residents 49; conditions for 3, 19, 23; 39; Institutional Cases 26; institutional structure 42; public attention 2; theorizing 24; *see also* violence

family 61: activism 55: alternate models of care 94, 96–7, 100; Chapman 60; communication with residents 33; Eichmann 58; foster care 98–9; incorporation of disabled persons in 21; Institutional Cases 26; institutional residents as 60, 63; lack of support 71, 86; research team 80; separation from 88; services 35; of staff 56, 62, 66; stigma 81; touring HRC 16, 92; violence 59; visits to residents 6, 49, 54, 71, 72; *see also* Geel (Belgium)
feeble-mindedness 5, 7–9
feeding 28, 34, 41, 85, 87–8, 100; forced 28–9; *see also* food; eating
food: as basic need 44; breakfast 85–6, 92; (institutional) control over 43, 44, 45, 83, 86; dinner 86, 100; emotional importance of 86, 87; food banks 86; *institutional muscle memory* 85, 86; lunch 45, 85–6; pets 87–8; (lack of) pleasure 85, 86, 100; poor quality 31, 86; preparation of 87; production of 11; and punishment 1, 29; at workshops 87; *see also* eating; feeding; meals
Foucault, M. 80–2; *see also* biopower

Geel (Belgium): boarders 97–9; City of Fools 97; foster families 97–9, 101
generosity 100
genocide 58, 64
Godemont, M.M.L. 97–8
Goffman, E. 3–4, 20, 40, 80–2
Goldstein, J.L. 97–9
Government of Ontario 1, 8, 13, 26, 61–2, 67

112   *Index*

hair 43, 77, 83–5, 93
Hamilton, F.C. 12
harassment 28
healing 76, 77, 88, 99
Heckert, C. 23
hitting 28, 49, 72, 77
Hlady, M. 18, 77
Holocaust 58, 64–6
"hot" violence *see* violence
humanity: crime against 64; erasure of
    41, 46, 54; limits of 50; questioned 41;
    reluctance to acknowledge 34; shared
    101–2; *see also* inhumanity
humanness 41
humiliation: example 45; fear of 83; in
    legal claims 70; as method of control
    50; punishment 55; physical 28–30;
    public 44; routine 1; surveillance 44;
    verbal 3, 28
Huronia Regional Centre (HRC)
    10, 77: cemetery 75; closing of 56;
    in court cases 35, 56, 65, 72–3,
    75; deinstitutionalization of 13;
    formerly Orillia Asylum for Idiots 7;
    grounds 67, 71, 93; history of 67,
    74; "playroom" 78; punishment 17;
    residents 1, 19, 27, 67, 70; solitary
    confinement in 48; staff 61; survivors
    13, 72, 89; total institution 1, 8, 75;
    underground tunnel in 51; *see also*
    architecture; buildings; cemetery;
    residents; staff; survivors
hygiene 41, 44, 46, 81, 83

idiocy 68, 73
idiots 5, 7–8
immigrants 2
incarceration: abolition of disability
    incarceration 73; act of violence
    39–40; death 50; experiences of 39–40,
    88, 90, 92; at HRC 19–20; *institutional
    objectification* 29; as marginalization
    32; population 34, 36–7; punitive 2
Indigenous peoples 2, 59, 75
indignity 54, 62; *see also* dignity
individuality: accountability 75; ceding
    to uniformity 83; embodied 85;
    encouraging 95, 99, 101; negation
    of 40, 41, 43, 46; refusal to erase 55;
    reproducing logic of institutional
    organization 79; tastes 87; *see also*
    dehumanization
inhumanity 98; *see also* humanity
injuries 14, 26, 28, 41, 69–72, 75

injustice 80: countering 87; experience of
    73, 83; frustration over 62; recounting
    instances of 65–6, 75; structural
    inequalities 67, 73; *see also* justice
Institutional Cases: allegations 31;
    definition 14, 19, 26, 28; examples
    27, 28; importance of 19, 37;
    reckoning with history of abuse 27;
    patterns and themes in 29, 35; tool
    of civil litigation 23
institutionalization: abusive conditions
    61; alternatives to 97; burden of 2;
    care 11; dehumanization 34–5, 40–1,
    73; Goffman 81; harm 69; history
    of 3, 4, 97; inherently violent 67, 75;
    injustice 102; isolation 63, 88; *logic* of
    79; legal material 14, 23, 27, 28, 32, 56;
    long-term effects of 20, 74, 79, 89, 90;
    necessity of 11; objective of 7;
    populations 6, 7, 13, 21, 29, 32–3;
    pressure to end 13; problem of 19;
    reoccurrence 73; resistance 81, 83;
    stories of 15, 18, 76; surviving 55, 79;
    theorizing 82; violence 26–7, 39, 43,
    50, 57, 66; *see also* dehumanization;
    deinstitutionalization
institutional model 46, 51, 102: austerity
    31–2, 35; efficiency 31–2, 54–5
institutional violence: alternatives
    to 98; Arendt 20, 56; Bandura 23;
    the body 83; "cold" 42; conditions
    for 2, 23, 24, 27, 46, 59; culture
    of 34, 41, 55, 66, 94; definition 3;
    dehumanization 25–6, 39, 40, 41;
    embodied 21; ethos of 23, 46, 50;
    expression of biopower 83; Goffman
    40; and history of disability 2; "hot"
    52; HRC example 8, 14, 19; inherent
    component of institutionalization
    67, 75, 94; instrumental functions
    of 30; legal analysis of 19, 20; lived
    experience of 13; long-term effects 2,
    3, 21, 92; Malacrida 40; practices of
    39; responses to 61, 72; routine 2, 43;
    scholarly literature on 3, 13, 23; staff
    perception of 56; survivors of 60, 67,
    79, 90, 92; theorizing 14, 19–20, 23–4,
    39–40, 55, 63; thoughtlessness 66;
    ubiquity of 1, 2, 3, 27, 55; Zimbardo
    40; *see also* abuse; sexual assault;
    situational violence; violence
Institut Raymond-Dewar 5
instrumental violence *see* violence
integration 11, 73, 89, 97–8, 101

Index 113

integrity 40, 79–80
isolation 87–8: in death 54; geographical
7, 9–11, 33, 37, 74, 89; as institutional
model 5–7, 9–11, 34, 63, 72; physical
17, 32–5, 47; as punishment 47; social
6, 33, 37, 55, 74, 89; *see also* solitary
confinement

Jaspers, K. 64
justice: Arendt 65; class action lawsuits
20, 65; corrective 14; disability 14;
failure of 67; limits of legal 21, 72,
73; requires other forms of care 3;
search for 13, 40, 65, 76; sticker 12;
system 15; *see also* injustice

König, Dr. K. 94–5
Koskie Minsky law firm 69, 76 n2
K-Zetnik 65–6

labour *see* patient labour
language: access to 21; creative 18; Nazi
64; passive 71; settlement 67, 70, 73;
sign 6, 30; terminology 5, 37 n1; United
Nations 74; *see also* terminology
L'Arche: communities 55, 96–8,
100–102; movement 21
laundry 11, 32, 43–4
law 63–6, 68
Law Commission of Canada (LCC) 73, 75
legal analysis 13, 19, 20, 66:
decision-making 26; instruments
20, 57; reports 26; research methods
14–15, 26
legal discourse *see* discourse
legal history 28
legal proceedings 13, 66: case law 3, 8,
26–7, 32, 37, 69; civil litigation 23, 26;
Tort litigation 14, 72; *see also* class
action lawsuit
legislation 73
life-sharing 94, 100–1
loneliness 79, 87–9

McIntyre v Ontario 27, 29, 31–2
Malacrida, C. 1, 40–1, 71–3, 82–3
meals 32, 80, 85, 100–1; *see also* eating;
feeding; food
medical discourse *see* discourse
medication 28, 49, 69, 71, 75, 87; *see also*
overmedication
mens rea 64
mental deficiency 8–9, *68*
mental retardation *see* idiocy; idiots

Michener Institute 40, 71, 73, 82
Migone, C. 18, 77
Milgram, S. 24
moral abdication: Bandura 28, 36;
conditions for 19, 28–9, 32, 34, 37, 39;
culture of 23; in practice 19; reframing
moral disengagement 26; situational
violence 19
morality 7, 20, 24–6, 30, 60:
moral agency 20, 25–7; moral
abandonment 23, 25–6, 28–9, 34;
moral abdication 19, 23, 26, 28–9,
32, 34; moral accountability 37;
moral character 71; moral codes
3, 25; moral compass 25; moral
disengagement 24–6; moral failing
25; moral reasoning 25–6, 30; moral
self-regulation 26, 34; moral subject
25; theory of 25
mythologization 20, 56, 64–6

nakedness *see* nudity
narratives: backlash against 62;
challenges of cohesion 18; group 18,
20; limits in courtrooms 66; as method
of legal research 14, 16, 19, 20, 39;
reference to time 61; of violence 55, 61
Nazism 7, 58–9, 64–5, 94
neglect: discourse 32, 71, 73; efforts
to resist 79; experiences of 19; as
institutional violence 3; in legal cases
1, 5, 23, 70–3; at Orillia's Hospital
School 12; as path to abuse 6, 74;
spaces of 72; theorizing 24, 80; result
of punishment 41
negligence 8, 31, 65
noise 79
non-consensual behaviour 43, 70
nudity 25, 30, 71: forced 28, 77;
nakedness 43, 45, 53, 70, 77

Oak Ridge (Penetanguishene Mental
Health Centre) 28, 30, 33, 36
obedience 46, 59
oral histories 3, 13, 19, 71
organizational elements: dynamics 24;
factors 23–4, 28; models of care 94;
norms 2, 21; orientation 31; practices
19, 23; structure 3, 21, 23–4, 26, 42,
79; traits 21, 28, 83, 94, 98
Orillia Asylum for Idiots 5, 7–9, *10*
Orillia's Hospital School 7, 9–12
orphanages 1, 9
orphans 2, 9

114 Index

overcrowding: causes of 12; chronic 8, 9, 74; failure to address 14; institutional design 5–6, 11–12, 31, 69, 70–2, 84; privacy 88; response to 8

overmedication 49–50; *see also* medication

Park, D.C. 5–12

patient labour: unremunerated 10–11, 31–2, 52, 69, 71, 88

performativity 82–3

pets: cats 88; dogs 88; *see also* staff pets

play 41, 50, 101

playroom 11, 44, 50, 77, *78*

political philosophy 20, 56, 63

post-traumatic stress disorder (PTSD) 2, 15; *see also* trauma

power: Arendt 57–8; Benjamin 57; the body 80, 81; of eugenics movement 7; Foucault 80–2; imbalances 63; justifying abuse of 62; levels of 27; masculinity 91; Mills 57; operations of 29, power over 60; productive 81; relations 58; relation to violence 57, 58; sharing 95; structures 31, 83; theorizing 57; transforming 93; Weber 57; *see also* biopower; disempower

prisons 2, 5, 28, 35, 71, 82

public apology: to staff 61, 63; to survivors 14, 66, 69–70, 89

punching 28, 88

punishment: alternatives to 100; between residents 49, 55; with dead bodies 54; degradation 1, 44, 50; "digging worms" 1, 47; care model 4, 16, 44, 47–9, 51–2, 55; euphemisms 25, 62; "hot" violence 52; humiliation 55, 83–4; in law 64, 70; for misbehaving 48, 75, 91; motivations for 6, 29, 30, 44, 46–7, 53; physical 6, 29, 41, 44; rape 53; threat of death 50; "warm" violence 46, *see also* food; humiliation; isolation; solitary confinement; violence

rape 3, 53

rebellion 58, 83–4

Recounting Huronia research project 15–16, 21, 39, 76; *see also* ethnographic methodologies

refugees 2

research dyads 16, 18

residential facilities 4, 8–13, 33, 73

residential schools 6, 32–3, 75

residents: abuse 6, 29, 33, 36, 41, 92; allegations of abuse 62, 69, 72; alternative models of care for 94, 99, 101; compliance 29, 30, 88; control over 34, 35, 43–4, 49, 83–6, 98; dead 54; dehumanization 34–5, 36, 39–41, 43, 54; de-institutionalization 13; fighting among 52; former 1, 18, 23, 30, 89; health 11, 44; humiliation 44; individuality 46, 54; institutional conditions 31, 32, 37; isolation 16–17, 32–33, 54, 72, 88, 100; justifying violence against 62; legal action 14, 26–7, 30, 66–7, 69–71; legal representatives 13; long-term effects of residential status 71; punishment 1, 44, 47–8, 50, 55; relationship to institution and staff 29, 30, 60, 62; restraint 59–60; segregation of 7; Seth 27; sexual abuse 52–3; Slark 27; social hierarchy 49; social valuation of 31, 32, 91, 101; staff perception of 63; surveillance 4, 44, 45–6; threats 50; violence against 2, 3, 20, 23, 26–8, 33; violence of 3, 41, 47–9, 51–2, 88, 98; welfare institutions 9; witnessing violence 52; *see also* family; patient labour; staff; survivors; violence

resilience 79, 92–3

resistance: embodied 21, 36, 77, 79, 81–3, 93; *see also* embodiment

restraint 6, 57, 59–60: of movement 33; physical 30; social 42

Rideau Regional Centre 13, 27, 32, 35–6, 61–3

Sansome, S. 61–3

Schedule 1 facilities: definition 13; history of 62; Institutional Cases 14, 31; isolation of 33; legal action 27, 29, 31, 35; narratives 61; reports on 32, 56

Section A claims 69, 72

Section B claims 69, 70, 72

sedation 30

Seed v Ontario 27–9, 32–3, 36

sensory deprivation *see* deprivation

Seth, P.: experience of institutionalization 76; inspiration 92; as plaintiff 13, 27, 29, 56, 67; punishment 75; regarding settlement 65; straightjacket 78

settlement: agreement 16, 27, 67, 69–70; disability justice 14; discourse 20, 67, 70, 73, 74; dissatisfaction with 65, 75;

Index 115

as opportunity for connection 89; packages 21, 27, 29, 67, 69–70, 90; process 21; public attention 14, 61; model of 27–8; *see also Dolmage v Ontario*; Slark
sexual assault: 1, 6, 28, 53–4, 70, 90; torture 52; violence 1, 53–4, 90; *see also* rape; torture; violence
shame 44–5, 88, 90–1
shaving 43, 84–5
Shilling, C. 80–1
shower 35, 43, 45–6, 92
sign language *see* language
situational moral disengagement 19, 23
slapping 28–9, 49, 57
Slark, M. 13, 27–9, 56, 65, 67, 75–6
sleep: as basic need 44; control of 4, 31, 33, 44, 46, 83; routines 19, 34, 41; schedules 29
sneaking up on residents 28, 36
Simmons, H.G. 7–10
situational violence: alternative models of care 21; Arendt 59; 'bad apple' behaviour 24; Bandura 23, 24; on continuum 41; facilitation of 26; Goffman 40; resistance of 93; theory 19; Wieviorka 39, 40, 42; Zimbardo 24, 40–41; *see also* Institutional Cases
social discourse *see* discourse
solitary confinement 28–30, 33, 47, 48, 52, 77 *see also* isolation
sound 18, 77, 79
spirituality 88, 94–6, 100
staff: abdication of responsibility for abusive actions 34, 59, 62–3; abusing residents 52, 84; access to residents 37, 45; administrative 12; controlling residents 34, 43, 44–5, 49, 83, 86; dehumanizing residents 35, 36, 60; disciplining residents 29; discouraging family visits 9, 72; favouritism 49; "hot" violence 51; humiliating residents 1, 28, 44, 47, 50; inciting fights between residents 49, 53; inflicting physical pain on residents 28, 36, 49; lack of oversight 31; legal action against 28; medical 30; memories about 18; motivations 30; mythologizing impulse 66; need for 11; oral histories and accounts 13, 20, 52, 56, 61; overworked 11; perspectives of 20, 34, 36, 56, 61–3; public apology to 61, 63; punishing residents 6, 29, 47, 49, 54, 91; relationships to residents 29, 60, 62–3, 66, 87; responsibilities 30, 32; schedules 29; thoughtlessness 60; threats 50; touring HRC grounds 16; underpaid 10; un(der)qualified 32, 33; violence or disrespect against 3, 47; *see also* 'bad apple' behaviour; staff pets; understaffing
staff pets 49
Stanford Prison Experiments 24
starvation 28, 44
Stead, D. 62
Steiner, R. 21, 95
stigma 74, 80–1, 89–90
strait jackets 48, 77, 78
subjectivity 41, 54, 82
surveillance 4, 40–1, 43–6, 53, 82, 101
survivors: abuse 49, 52, 61, 77; activism 55, 75; Befus 82; food 87; histories 16, 80; Holocaust 64, 65; language 71, 72; legal action 1, 8, 13–14, 15, 67, 71–2; life after institutionalization 86, 88–90, 92; medical diagnoses 15; narratives 16, 55–6, 61–3, 66, 77; public responsibility towards 102; punishment 46, 54; *Recounting Huronia* research project 15–16, 18–19, 39, 42, 60–1, 76; registry 14; researcher relationship with 80, 86; resistance 79, 82, 83; in service of 59; Seth 13, 75; settlement 21; Slark 13, 75; stories 1, 13, 18–20, 23, 27, 40; surveillance 44–5; testimony 20–1, 56, 62, 65–6, 72, 83; understanding 4; violence against 20, 21, 27–8; visiting HRC 54; voices 79; *see also* food; Huronia Regional Centre; residents; Seth, P.; Slark, M.

teenagers *see* youth
Templin v HMQ 27, 36
terminology 5, 70; *see also* language
therapy 30: 'coercive milieu therapy' 35; therapeutic benefits or intent 10, 14, 34
thoughtlessness 20, 56, 58, 60, 62, 66
threats 7, 96: of death 50; of punishment 49
throwing objects 28–9, 36, 47, 49
Tort litigation *see* legal proceedings
torture 24, 30, 41, 52; *see also* sexual assault
total institutions 1, 3–4, 8, 20–1, 40
trauma: accounts of 16, 20, 21, 28, 39–40, 89; collective 14; embedded 79,

116 *Index*

89; flashbacks 88; hierarchicalization of 21, 73, 75; institutionalization 59, 75, 90; memory 65; monetization of 73; repressed memory 1, 21; re-traumatization 21, 61, 67, 71, 79, 88–90; *see also* post-traumatic stress disorder
treatments *see* curative treatments

understaffing 14, 31, 33, 43, 69, 71: chronic 11
uniformity 83–4, 99
United States 3–4, 8, 10

Vanier, J. 21, 96, 99
victim 36, 63, 88: affect 20, 57, 63; blaming 26, 36
violence: as care 20, 56; "cold" 40, 41–2, 46, 53, 55, 58; deep 24, 37, 39, 54, 94; dehumanization 36; extraordinary (explosive) 41; "hot" 39–42, 51–3, 58; inevitability of 55, 57; instrumental 30, 37, 39–40, 42, 46, 57–8; moral 25; Nazism 59, 64; ordinary (quotidian) 41, 57; rationale for 5, 24, 30, 35; through medicine 49; sadistic 55; spectrum 41, 55, 58; symbolic 54–5; towards residents 1, 51; *violent milieus*

24; "warm" 46, 53; Zimbardo 24; *see also* institutional violence; situational violence
voice 18, 72, 79, 92
Voronka, J. 10

walls: architecture 32; confinement 79; feeding through 34; hallucinations 99; institutional 11, 27, 55, 86; speaking to 18, 45, 77, 79; *see also* architecture
"warm" violence *see* violence
washing 32, 34, 45–6, 74, 91
weight *see* body
Welch Report 31, 62
Welsh v Ontario 27, 29–30, 33, 35–6
Wieviorka, M. 39–42, 58
Williston Report 31–3, 35, 62, 69, 75
Williston, W.B. 5–6, 8, 10–12, 31–2, 69
workshops *see* ethnographic methodologies
Wright, D. 5–7, 9
W. Ross MacDonald School for the Blind 5, 27, 29, 33, 36
Wynne, K. 70, 89

youth 7, 9, 32, 59, 73

Zimbardo, P. 24, 40, 41

Printed in the United States
by Baker & Taylor Publisher Services